# MISSION POSSIBLE

# Marian Schindler
# Robert Schindler, M.D.

While this book is designed for your personal profit
and enjoyment, it is also intended for group study.
A Leader's Guide with Victor Multiuse Transparen-
cy Masters is available from your local bookstore or
from the publisher.

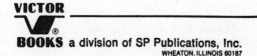

**VICTOR**
**BOOKS** a division of SP Publications, Inc.
WHEATON, ILLINOIS 60187

*Offices also in*
Whitby, Ontario, Canada
Amersham-on-the-Hill, Bucks, England

Permission for cartoons from *SIM Now,* SIM International.

Unless otherwise noted, Scripture quotations are from the *Holy Bible: New International Version* © 1978 by the New York International Bible Society. Used by permission of Zondervan Bible Publishers. Other Scriptures are from the *King James Version* (KJV).

Recommended Dewey Decimal Classification: 266
    Suggested Subject Heading: MISSIONS

Library of Congress Catalog Card Number: 83-51308
ISBN: 0-88207-618-3

VICTOR BOOKS
A division of SP Publications, Inc.
    Wheaton, Illinois 60187

# Contents

Foreword    **5**

1 Mission Motivation    **7**

2 God's Plan for Missions    **14**

3 Missions of the Past    **26**

4 The Next Step—Mission Strategy    **39**

5 Qualified Personnel Needed    **54**

6 New on the Job?    **70**

7 Mission Methods    **84**

8 Ministries of Concern    **96**

9 Missions from the Non-Western World    **109**

10 The Wall of Islam    **119**

11 Interference from the Communist Voice    **132**

12 The Sending Church    **146**

13 Where in the World Do You Fit In?    **157**

Bibliography    **165**

Robert and Marian Schindler served as missionaries with the Sudan Interior Mission for 13 years. Bob is the founder of the ELWA Hospital in Liberia, West Africa. The Schindlers were decorated by the Liberian government with distinctions in the Humane Order of African Redemption.

They presently live in Stevensville, Michigan where Bob is a general surgeon. His partnership in a group practice makes it possible to serve short terms with missions. Bob is president-elect of the Christian Medical Society. Marian is active in neighborhood Bible studies and Christian Women's Club. They frequently speak and teach about missions in local churches. The Schindlers have two sons, Robert and John.

# Foreword

World evangelization—the announcement of God's saving love—is central to an understanding of Christian faith. It is not an optional matter that one embraces or discards. But many people who claim to be followers of Christ don't know that. They have come to faith out of personal need and have discovered just how effective Gospel Power is. Gospel Power releases people from guilt, fills them with hope, energizes them with power, and draws them into new and healthy relationships.

But while many have found Gospel Power, they may have missed the fact of Gospel Responsibility. And that's where world evangelization enters the picture. The responsibility of the Christian in world evangelization is a matter of discipleship and obedience.

In this book, Bob and Marian Schindler have taken the profound topic of world evangelization and strained it through their own experience. They have provided not only a series of insights into the Scriptures but have shown us how they dealt with the ideas.

My wife, Gail, and I have stood at Dr. Bob's side as he performed surgery on a number of African patients at the ELWA Hospital in Monrovia, Liberia. We have watched as he worked with a staff of medical aides, most of whom he personally trained. We have listened to him pray for a patient before anesthesia was administered. Outside the OR, we have watched Marian interacting with Liberians of all ages who were drawn to Christ because of her servanthood character.

Because I know that this book is stamped with the authenticity of personal performance, it is a privilege for me to introduce Bob and Marian Schindler to the many Christians who will study *Mission Possible.*

As you come into contact with two genuine followers of Christ who've done world evangelism, you will see in a fresh way the importance not only of experiencing Gospel Power but also of exercising Gospel Responsibility.

Gordon MacDonald
Lexington, Massachusetts   1983

To all our friends with whom we worked
at the ELWA Hospital in past years
and to those who continue so faithfully
to serve our Lord Jesus Christ there today

# 1

# Mission Motivation

"Why in the world did you ever want to go to Liberia?" That question has come to us over and over again, from people in many different places. And depending on who is asking, it is often a difficult question to answer.

For instance, we'll probably be more careful in framing our answer for a skeptic or for someone who doesn't understand the language we so often use in missions. But that may be to the good—perhaps we are more honest when we can't give pat answers!

Why did we want to go to Liberia? That deals with motivation. We need to be motivated for anything we do, and motivations are difficult to sort out! Many times there is a mixture of motives in why we do what we do.

We left for Liberia on the evening of October 12, 1962. As our Pan Am jet took off over the fairyland lights of New York City, we felt like we were diving off a high diving board. There was no turning back. The next morning as we descended, we looked down on the thatch-roofed villages of the rain forest. When we landed, the windows were steamy with the humidity of the tropics. We stepped out of the plane with our two little boys, Bob Jr., who had just turned four, and John, only two. What had made us go to Liberia?

Bob was born in the neat little Swiss-German community of Berne, Indiana. He spent the first few weeks of his life in a shoe box, for he was a preemie, weighing only three and one-half pounds. At the age of 11, Bob found it easy to put his faith in Jesus Christ. He came from a Christian family, and the community had a godly heritage. There were five churches, and other activities automatically shut down on Wednesday evenings so that everyone in Berne could go to prayer meeting.

Bob went on to Wheaton College with the vision of becoming a doctor and returning to Berne to practice. His premed studies meant he had to keep at the books. After his second year of college, he was invited to take a year off and go with a Wheaton quartet as their bass to travel with Jack Wyrtzen and also sing on the Word of Life Hour radio broadcast. That's where he met Marian Wilson, a student at Taylor University. She was working at Word of Life Camp in the Adirondacks. It was a summer romance that never died!

Marian was from a South Dakota farming community, where she had grown up in a Christian family. She too had put her faith in Christ in her youth. From Taylor University, it was a big move for her to go all the way to the East Coast.

It was during those years at college and in youth work that both of us began to deal with some important information we kept hearing about God and missions. Our minds, emotions, and wills were challenged. This information helped to shape our motivations for going to Liberia.

We began to understand more about the mission of God, the fact that He has a plan, as revealed in the Word of God. That He created man in His image and desires to have fellowship with him. That man has broken this fellowship by sin. We could not get away from the truth that God is seeking to bring all men to Himself. It is His mission to reconcile man to Himself through Jesus Christ His Son.

We became more aware of world needs which seemed so overwhelming in comparison to opportunities in America. We began to ask, "Why in the world can't we go?" As we look back now on our motivations, we can see that we were in part satisfying our own need for self-fulfillment. There is a real sense of purpose in missions, a big cause to join. Doing something really worthwhile in life might be some of the motivation. Certainly, our own needs play a part in motives. But there is much more.

## Response to Human Needs

Part of missionary motivation is our awareness of the needs of others. Coming out of medical school and a surgery residency, Bob was motivated by the medical needs of the world. He heard of countries where only half of the children made it to age five. He read of malnutrition, malaria, dehydration, and tropical illnesses. He saw a suffering world in need of help.

Word from Liberia confirmed this need. Nurses, most of them wives of the radio personnel at ELWA radio station, had

Figure 1

started a small clinic but were soon overwhelmed with the work. They prayed for a doctor and a hospital to help meet the needs of the community.

Once we arrived, we were always reminded of the medical needs. In the middle of the night there might be a knock on the door, and Bob would hear the shrill cry of a baby deathly ill with cerebral malaria. Looking out, he'd see more than 20 people, some with lanterns, coming from the village with the concerned mother. Or he might be called to the bush area reserved for childbirth, where no other man was allowed, to assist in a difficult delivery. The needs were overwhelming, and we knew that a hospital would help.

Others ·in missions are motivated by the need of educa-tion around the world. Low literacy rates are a challenge to teachers.

There are the obvious material needs too, with the great contrast between the haves and the have-nots of the world. Most countries do not have the affluence of the Western world—air conditioners, cars, beautiful homes, abundant food. We heard a good definition of wealth at an Urbana Missionary Convention. Wealth is having options: Which shirt shall I wear? Which pair of shoes? What is my choice on the menu? Options. Part of missionary motivation is a desire to share material benefits with others, to help them develop ways to raise their own standard of living.

The awareness of needs—physical, intellectual, material—can all be part of going. There is a desire to physically help the suffering world. There is a desire to help others improve their lives. There is a desire to do good. All of these motives can be factors in going with the message of the Gospel, but standing by themselves, they are weak.

## Response to Spiritual Needs

A stronger motivation in missions is an awareness of the spiri-tual needs of others. There are millions who have never even heard the name of Jesus. Missiologists tell us that nearly three out of four people in the world today have not heard the Gospel in an adequate way. And yet, Scripture tells us that they must hear!

Consistent with His plan, God is working to bring man back to fellowship with Him. The Bible says, "All have sinned and fall short of the glory of God," and "The wages of sin is death; but the gift of God is eternal life in Christ Jesus our Lord" (Rom. 3:23; 6:23). Scripture teaches the reality of hell and eternal separation from God for man in his sin. But God has provided the way to be saved.

J. Herbert Kane reminds us,

God's love makes it possible for the repentant sinner to be saved. God's holiness makes it inevitable that the unrepentant sinner will perish. Both are part of the Gospel; both are part of the mandate. Without the love of God, we would not have the Gospel. Without the wrath of God, we would not need the Gospel (*Understanding Christian Missions,* Baker, p. 119).

Jesus Himself said, "I am the way and the truth and the life. No one comes to the Father except through Me" (John 14:6).

Peter testified, "Salvation is found in no one else, for there is no other name under heaven given to men by which we must be saved" (Acts 4:12). And Paul reasoned:

"Everyone who calls on the name of the Lord will be saved." How, then, can they call on the one they have not believed in? And how can they believe in the one of whom they have not heard? And how can they hear without someone preaching to them? And how can they preach unless they are sent? (Rom. 10:13-15)

Kane says, "This is logic, not rhetoric; and the logic is devastating" (*Understanding Christian Missions,* p. 102). How can they call? How can they believe? How can they hear? Part of missionary motivation is the awareness that they *must* hear.

We all look forward to a day when a cure for cancer will be found. Will the news of this cure be kept a secret? No! Can you imagine the excitement as the news media flash the message around the world? You can picture the swift action on the part of the medical profession to make the cure available to all who need it. It would be the only logical way to respond.

A motivation for missions is the awareness of the need for others to hear the good news of the Gospel of Jesus Christ. Part of our own motivation to go outside of the United States was the fact that there are so many more opportunities to hear the Gospel here—more than anywhere else in the world. To us, the need seemed greater in Liberia.

## Response to God's Command
But there is a stronger motivation than response to human needs. As Christians, we should want to obey the commands of Jesus Christ. One's last words are not usually easily forgotten, and Christ's last command, to take the Gospel into all the world, is found in all four Gospels and also in Acts. Obedience to His commands is a strong motivation in missions.

Then Jesus came to them and said, "All authority in heaven and on earth has been given to Me. Therefore go and make disciples of all nations, baptizing them in the name of the Father and of the Son and of the Holy Spirit, and teaching them to obey everything I have commanded you. And surely I will be with you always, to the very end of the age" (Matt. 28:18-20).

He said to them, "Go into all the world and preach the Good News to all creation" (Mark 16:15).

Then He opened their minds so they could understand the Scriptures. He told them, "This is what is written: The Christ will suffer and rise from the dead on the third day, and repentance and forgiveness of sins will be preached in His name to all nations, beginning at Jerusalem. You are witnesses of these things" (Luke 24:45-48).

Again Jesus said, "Peace be with you! As the Father has sent Me, I am sending you" (John 20:21).

But you will receive power when the Holy Spirit comes on you; and you will be My witnesses in Jerusalem, and in all Judea and Samaria, and to the ends of the earth" (Acts 1:8).

## Response to God's Love

The strongest motivation for missions is the love of God. John said, "We love Him, because He first loved us" (1 John 4:19, KJV). Can we begin to know the all-encompassing love of God that reaches around us and around the world? Can we begin to realize that He is not willing that any should perish, but that all should come to repentance? (2 Peter 3:9)

It is God's love that sent Jesus to take our place and to die for our sins. Now we are invited to follow Jesus, to deny ourselves, and move out to do His will. He says, "If you love Me, you will obey what I command" (John 14:15).

Obeying His commands, because of a growing appreciation of His love and an understanding of His will, is what puts quality into mission motivation. The motivating love of God should increase in importance for the missionary—and for every Christian. As we follow Him, His love for the world becomes our love for the world. We act out of obedience to His command because we love Him.

While visiting Chicago a few years ago, we attended Moody Church and heard Dr. Warren W. Wiersbe give a message on missions. He said, "We have the Message, we have the Money, we have the Manpower, and we have the Methods to accomplish the work of evangelization of the world. But our Motivation is questionable."

Well, we have answered the question, "Why in the world did you ever want to go to Liberia?" Now it's our turn to ask you, "Why in the world are you where you are today? What is *your* motivation to get in on God's mission to evangelize the world and make disciples of all nations?"

# 2

# God's Plan for Missions

There is a plan for the world. It originated with God. But He shares the blueprints in the Word of God. We read:

> For God so loved the world that He gave His one and only Son, that whoever believes in Him shall not perish but have eternal life. For God did not send His Son into the world to condemn the world, but to save the world through Him (John 3:16-17).

The details for the plan are worked out as people follow Jesus' command: "Go into all the world and preach the Good News to all creation" (Mark 16:15). His plan is being carried out. There are more people receiving the Good News today than ever before in history!

In Africa we see the Book of Acts in action, for the church there is now a sending church. Church growth experts tell us that the church in Africa is growing at the phenomenal rate of an estimated 20,000 per day. Latin America is not far behind.

Those who visit South Korea tell of some of the most effective churches in the world. In Seoul, where most church buildings were leveled in the Korean War, some 2,000 evangelical churches have been built. The largest church in the world, the Full Gospel Central Church with 250,000 members, is in South

Korea. Christians in that country are witnessing Christians. At five o'clock each morning the church chimes call Christians to prayer.

Word came of reopened churches in China, and of those who wait in line to get into the churches. It was Sister Claire who gave us a glimpse of the church of Jesus Christ in China, in an experience we will never forget. It was through Christian Chinese-American friends that we met her. Ray and Lucy came to the United States as students from Hong Kong and became Christians through a Chinese Christian group at the University of Michigan. When job opportunities brought them to western Michigan, they joined our church in Stevensville. They also became American citizens. It was exciting to see their interest in the opening up of China.

One day Ray and Lucy introduced us to their friend David. He told us that his aunt had recently come from China and was a guest in his home. He invited us to come meet her that afternoon.

On the way to the apartment, we recalled how in recent years we had actually wondered if there were any Christians left in China. It was almost embarrassing to think of all the missionaries who had once worked there and then not to hear anything of a church in China. We wondered just what kind of a Christian we were going to meet. When David opened the door, standing right behind him was Sister Claire, eager to meet us. She must have been in her 70s, but her coal-black hair and the lively twinkle in her eyes belied that. She was dressed in the typical gray trousers and blouse of China. We were greeted so warmly by this Christian lady that we felt at ease, as if we had known her for years. As we conversed for two hours, it was easy to forget that we were talking through an interpreter, her nephew, David.

She radiated the love and joy of Christ as she spoke softly. She seemed to be smiling all the time, and soft chuckles accented her joy as she spoke of the Lord's goodness—"The way of the cross is hard, but God's mercy and goodness are so rich." The conversation stopped for a moment as she quietly wept when she spoke of her fellow workers and their hardships and persecutions in years past.

Back in the 1930s, after attending a Methodist school where she had become a Christian, she joined a group of women providing medical care to the poor in the rural area of north-west China. She said, "Like the Apostle Paul, we worked with our hands, fed ourselves, and spread the Gospel." Later we learned that she was a medical doctor.

Things changed when the Communists came into power. In speaking of them, she referred to Proverbs 21:1, "The King's heart is in the hand of the Lord; He directs it like a watercourse wherever He pleases."

She told of Christians who were faithful unto death: "In the difficult times, the persecution times, there are miracles which God performs for real Christians, and those non-Christians in China, even the Communist leaders, also see the glory of our Lord." She spoke of the growing respect for Christians.

She was in the United States to tell the church here of the Lord's faithfulness in China. She talked of the little family groups of three or four—the only way they could meet as Christians—who gathered together through the years, without theological institutions, without church buildings, without Bibles, but growing in their precious faith. She talked of the new opportunities for Christians to be more open, of the grow-ing number of believers, and of the hunger of the youth to know God. We got a glimpse of God's special people in that great land as Sister Claire smiled, as she wept, as she talked of the church in China, still very much alive and growing!

## The Mandate for Missions

When we hear of the church of Jesus Christ, alive and spread-ing around the world, we are encouraged. But there is another side. Statistics tell us that there are over four billion people on this globe. They also tell us that some three billion do not have adequate opportunity to hear the Good News of Jesus Christ. That's three out of four.

We were reminded of this side of the story when our son

John was a student at Taylor University. He called us one night to tell us about a chapel service that had really made an impression on him. Marilyn Laszlo, missionary to New Guinea with Wycliffe Bible Translators, had told the students of her work with the Sepik Iwam language group at a village called Hauna, where she had translated the Bible, or as they said, "carved God's talk on a banana leaf in their language."

One day some visitors came from another tribal village. They had heard of the good things happening at Hauna. One man who spoke Pidgin English was especially interested as Marilyn showed the visitors the church and told them, "The God we worship is everywhere, but this is His house where we come to sing praises and hear His Word. It is His talk we are carving on the banana leaf."

The visitors from the other village begged Marilyn to come to their village and carve God's talk in their language, but she knew that she still had much to do in Hauna. It would be years before their language could be translated.

But Marilyn could not forget their insistence. So before furlough, she and a companion set out one day, traveling by canoe back into the mountains, trekking through thick undergrowth and through the swamps, until finally they came to the village.

As they stepped into the clearing of the village, they saw one building in the center that was different from the other structures. Marilyn asked them, "What is that building?"

"Oh," the Pidgin-speaking man answered, "that is God's house."

"Oh?" Marilyn asked. "So a missionary has already come to preach God's Word?"

"No," was their reply.

"Then, why do you have this building?"

"Because we saw a building like this in your village where people hear about God, and so we built one too. We are waiting for someone to come and tell us about God in our own language."

Our 20-year-old John had a hard time telling us the rest. He said, "Marilyn told us that they are still waiting . . . waiting for someone to come and tell them." (See Clarence W. Hall's book, *Miracle on the Sepik,* Gift Publications, pp. 87-90.)

John was moved by this: *"They are still waiting to hear."* And we too are moved as we stop to consider that there are thousands and thousands of other villages across the world still waiting to hear. How will they hear?

The Bible is the revelation of God and of His will, and in it we see that God does have a plan. This is not just human speculation or a plan that man has devised to work his way to God. This is God's plan to reach a world of loved people.

In the beginning, God created a perfect world. He created man to enjoy it and rule over it. Man was to have fellowship with God, his Creator. But things went wrong when man chose to disobey God and to sin. The world has never been the same since then, because of God's judgment on sin.

We all fall under God's judgment. The Apostle Paul reminds us that no one is righteous, "not even one" (Rom. 3:10).

## The Message of Missions

But God still loves the world, and we see in the Bible that He does not want to leave the world in a lost condition. He has a plan. This is the message of missions.

It would be easy to assume that we Westerners all know this message, and yet that is far from true. If you listen to short-wave radio, you know that there are times when you can't quite make out the message. It sounds garbled. The same thing can happen to the message of the Gospel so that it does not come through as it should. It's important that we clarify the message.

On our first Christmas morning in Liberia, we were awakened at about three o'clock with joyful singing accompanied by the drumbeat, "Go, tell it on the mountain that Jesus Christ is born!"

That's the message of missions—"Jesus Christ is born!" God has made it possible for man to be saved from his sins and return to God through Jesus Christ. We crawled out of bed that

Christmas morning to greet a truckload of young Liberian Christians—and to be reminded again of this Good News!

The message begins with the basis for God's action: "For God so loved the world." This is good news to people governed by fear, controlled by superstitions, to people who worship evil spirits, or who believe in a supreme being who has no emotion. "For God so loved the world that He gave His one and only Son, that whoever believes in Him shall not perish but have eternal life" (John 3:16).

Paul explained it to the Corinthians, "For what I received I passed on to you as of first importance: that Christ died for our sins according to the Scriptures, that He was buried, that He was raised on the third day according to the Scriptures" (1 Cor. 15:3-4).

It is possible to return to God because Jesus Christ died for our sins. He rose again victorious over death and is at the right hand of God interceding for us! This Good News is the heart of the missionary message.

But a message calls for a response. Because man has a free will, God's invitation graciously extends to: "whoever believes" (John 3:16), "trusts in Him" (Rom. 10:11), and "calls on the name of the Lord" (Rom. 10:13). These people are the recipients of His gift of eternal life. Not only do people need to hear and understand the message; they must also respond to the message.

Those who do receive Jesus Christ find the message of missions expanded so that they might be discipled and grow in grace and knowledge of God.

## The Model for Missions

We are always looking for a pattern to follow, an example. Have you ever considered that the very nature of God—the Father, the Son, and Holy Spirit—is a model, a pattern of missionary reaching, sending, reconciling?

It was John R. W. Stott of England who so effectively pointed this out to us at an Urbana Missionary Convention sponsored by Inter-Varsity Christian Fellowship. We were at our first

Urbana convention in 1976, and were overwhelmed to see some 17,000 students gathered to consider Christian missions. These serious and sensitive young Christians were asking God what He would have them do in the world.

We still have the notes we took when John R. W. Stott spoke each morning, and we want to share some of his thoughts. He pointed out that the Living God is a Missionary God, the Lord Christ is a Missionary Christ, the Holy Spirit is a Missionary Spirit, and the Christian Church is a Missionary Church.

• The Living God is a God of Mission. He has a plan to be carried through for man's salvation and blessing. He entered into history to carry out this plan.

In the Old Testament, after the account of Creation and man's sin in the Garden of Eden with the resulting separation from God, God promised a way of redemption which was to come. It was through Abraham that God would make a great nation (Gen. 12:1-3). Through Abraham's descendants, "as numerous as the stars in the sky and as the sand on the seashore," would all nations be blessed (Gen. 22:17-18; Heb. 11:12). Have you ever tried to count the stars? Or the grains of sand on the seashore? We lived on the beach of the Atlantic Ocean in Liberia, and we would watch the sands wash in and out with the tide. But try to count the sands? Never.

Numberless descendants of Abraham—a great nation to be blessed and to be a blessing—how would this come about? In Galatians 3:29 we read: "If you belong to Christ, then you are Abraham's seed, and heirs according to the promise."

There it is! God carries out His mission, His plan, through His Son, Jesus Christ, and so His blessing will rest on a numberless throng! As John saw a vision of those who will stand before the throne of the Lamb, he viewed "a great multitude that no one could count, from every nation, tribe, people, and language" (Rev. 7:9). The multitude of those redeemed will be so great that no one can even count them! There will be those from the Old Testament times who by faith looked forward to the Promised Redeemer, and those since Christ's coming who by faith have received Him as their Saviour, and so belong to Him.

God created a world. He called a man. He promised a great nation, and through this nation, He sent His Son to fulfill the promise of blessing. The Living God is a Missionary God. He is not a distant being, aloof from mankind. He entered human history by sending His Son, Jesus Christ, to fulfill His mission.

John R. W. Stott reminded us that because our God is a global God, we need to become Christians with a global vision.

• In the Gospels we see the Lord Jesus as a Missionary Christ. Jesus was sent by the Father. In John 1:14 we read: "The Word became flesh and lived for a while among us. We have seen His glory, the glory of the one and only Son, who came from the Father, full of grace and truth."

Sent by His Father, He totally identified with those to whom He came. Jesus "being in very nature God, did not consider equality with God something to be grasped, but made Himself nothing, taking the very nature of a servant, being made in human likeness. And being found in appearance as a man, He humbled Himself and became obedient to death—even death on a cross!" (Phil. 2:6-8)

There's the pattern for Christian missionaries—identification with the people to whom they minister. To enter human culture, Jesus Christ was born as we all are. He lived among the common people, performing compassionate service. He went about doing good as He brought the message of reconciliation. He kept to His goal, obedience to death on the cross to reconcile the world unto God.

Then He passed His mission on to others: "As the Father has sent Me, I am sending you" (John 20:21).

• The Book of Acts tells of the Holy Spirit who was sent into the world to give believers power to be witnesses for Jesus Christ (Acts 1:8). The Holy Spirit was sent to convict and to convince. He was sent to minister to the church, to give instruction for growth. The Holy Spirit is a Missionary Spirit.

• There is yet another model in the Book of Acts and in the Epistles—a Missionary Church. John R. W. Stott pointed out that churches began as a product of mission, but that evangelized churches became evangelizing churches. The nature of the church of Jesus Christ is to spread—as love, salt, light—around the world. While the church is a family relationship, it is also an army to move out with the Good News. The church is the agent for God's worldwide mission. (Stott's messages can also be found in the book, *Declare His Glory,* ed. David M. Howard, InterVarsity, pp. 31-91.)

God the Father originated the mission to redeem man. He reached out to man. Jesus Christ was the Sent One who identified with those to whom He was sent. He came to reconcile the world unto God. The Holy Spirit was sent to give power for the mission. The church is the agent to carry out the mission. Therefore, Christians are to be a people of mission.

## The Means of Missions

As we look through the Book of Acts to see the story of early church growth, we notice how God used people to reach people. Perhaps there are other ways He could have worked, but the message is more effective when it comes from someone who has experienced it. God employs human agents to carry His message.

Do you recall how Philip, who was already busy for the Lord in Samaria, was directed to go into the desert to explain the Scripture to an Ethiopian whom he didn't even know? The Ethiopian was ready to receive Christ.

The Gola people in Liberia, West Africa were also ready to believe. Living in the interior of the country, most of them were spirit-worshipers, though Islam was also there. In the 1960s, missionary radio station ELWA beamed programs in their dialect into that area, and groups of believers sprang up here and there in Gola country. They realized that they needed to know more about this new life, so they gathered together in a town called Gondatown and sent a message to ELWA, "Please send us a missionary."

SIM's Arn Lueders went to see what had happened. He was warmly welcomed and was invited to stay with a James B. Ware. Amazed at what he found, Arn encouraged the believers and helped them form a local church. But because of the shortage of staff, he could not promise to send them a missionary. When Arn went back to ELWA, the Golas built a church and put a radio on the clay pulpit to listen to broadcasts in their language.

Ten years later, a survey team was sent from ELWA to look into church planting opportunities in that area. Needing a place to spend the night, they stayed with the same man who had welcomed Arn Lueders, James B. Ware. As they met for prayer that night, Mr. Ware pleaded that someone be sent to teach the Gola people the ways of God. He told them that in the beginning, nearly the whole village came to services. But since there was no one to teach them, the church had withered away until now there were only ten people.

Les Unruh, formerly a missionary to Ethiopia, was on that trip, and he was challenged to return to Gola country. Les recounted, "One man sat there and said, 'You know, we don't want to be Muslims. We want to be Christians, but nobody has come to teach us' " (Kerry Lovering, "Assignment: Gola," *Africa Now,* SIM, November-December 1979).

Today Les and Verla Unruh and others are working in the Gola area. The Means of Missions are human agents carrying the Gospel of Christ.

But there is another side to the means—the important ministry of the Holy Spirit. The disciples were told to wait to begin their mission until they received the power of the Holy Spirit. It is the Holy Spirit who guides in the direction to be taken—to individuals, to groups, and to locations. He gives the power. He brings the conviction of sin, the faith to believe, and the changed lives.

The Means of Missions: human agents empowered by the Holy Spirit.

## The Measure of Outreach

What if the disciples would have waited until Jerusalem was thoroughly evangelized and discipled before they moved out with the Gospel? We might still be waiting!

What is the measure of outreach in God's plan? Jesus Christ

told His disciples that the Gospel must be preached to all nations (Luke 24:47). He told them to carry the Good News to the ends of the earth (Acts 1:8). This is a global mission for which we need a global vision.

At an Urbana convention, we heard Argentine evangelist and missionary statesman, Luis Palau, tell how he got a world vision. He said, "I was brought up in a marvelous church, but we were self-centered. A missionary named Keith came to our town. One day he said to me, 'Luis, every Wednesday after work, why don't you come over and let's pray?' "

Now most young people could think of more exciting things to do than pray with a missionary, but Luis said, "OK."

The first Wednesday they got on their knees and the missionary prayed for Luis, for his family, and the local church, calling the elders by name.

The second Wednesday they prayed for the whole city of Cordoba where he lived, for each church and the leaders. Luis said he hadn't realized how many churches there were!

The following Wednesday, Keith had a map of the province of Cordoba with 900 cities and 90 evangelical churches. Luis said, "The prayer meetings were getting longer!"

The fourth Wednesday Keith had a map of Argentina, and they prayed province by province. Keith knew all the statistics. Luis said, "It was like getting on a jet and flying all over the country. I was getting excited!"

The fifth Wednesday it was a map of the Americas. Luis said that the prayer meetings continued each Wednesday, on through Europe, Asia, Africa, around the world. By the time Keith brought a map of the whole world, Luis had learned Christian vision. He had taken his eyes off of himself and was seeing the whole world. He said, "I saw what God wanted to do for the world, and that we too could get out and do something about it! Keith taught me vision!"

A big vision, a big outreach for a big world! According to God's plan, the outreach is the whole world. Yes, the God of mission plans that all should hear the Good News that He sent His Son, Jesus Christ, so that man might be brought back to

God. Are we a people of mission with a vision of the world that God wants to reach?

Is such a mission just too big a task? Is it even possible? It must be, because God planned it.

# 3

# Missions of the Past

A missionary working in Africa tells of the time he and his companions were on their way to preach in a village which had already been opened to the Gospel. But on their way through the jungle, they chose the wrong fork in the road, and ended up in another village where the people had never heard of Jesus Christ.

As the chief listened intently to their story of One who loved him and the people of his village, he asked the missionary, "Did your father know this story?"

"Oh, yes," the missionary replied, "my father knew."

"Well, then," the chief asked, "did your father's father know?"

"Oh, yes, he did," the missionary smiled and continued, "many of my people have known."

The chief looked at him intently for a moment and then asked, "You know the story, your father knew, your father's father knew the story. My father's father died. My father died. They never heard. This is the first that I've heard. You have come to tell us . . . but why has it taken so long?"

Why has it taken so long? Nearly 2,000 years ago Jesus Christ commissioned His followers to take the Gospel to the ends of the earth. A look at history will help us to understand how the Gospel has already been taken to much of the world, often in perilous conditions. Like a thread, the message of the Gospel has been woven through history, sometimes appearing to be weak but never breaking, as men and women through the ages have responded to Christ's command to preach the Gospel. In this quick overview, we will look at two eras—the early history of missions and the history of missions in the twentieth century.

## The Early History of Missions

Christian missions as we know them began at Pentecost. God had called out a people through the ages and then sent the One who had been promised, His Son Jesus Christ. The mission now was to tell others this Good News and to make disciples. Jesus gave these new missionary candidates their instructions just prior to His return to heaven. Then He told them to remain in Jerusalem to receive the power of the Holy Spirit before they ventured out on this new mission.

So they waited and in preparation for their task, they prayed together. On the Day of Pentecost, as the disciples were gathered together in Jerusalem, the Holy Spirit came upon them just as Jesus had promised. They were prepared to go.

• Explosive Expansion. Something amazing happened that day. The Bible tells us that they were able to speak to the people from many nations who had come to Jerusalem for Pentecost. Acts 2:4 says, "All of them were filled with the Holy Spirit and began to speak in other tongues as the Spirit enabled them."

An amazed and curious crowd from many different countries gathered around them and asked, "Are not all these men who are speaking Galileans? Then how is it that each of us hears them in his own native language?" (Acts 2:7-8)

Have you ever noticed the list of countries represented that day? The visitors were from such faraway places as Asia, Egypt, Libya, and Rome! Imagine their excitement as they exclaimed, "We hear them declaring the wonders of God in our own tongues!" (Acts 2:11)

What a commissioning service! Right there Peter had the

opportunity to preach the Gospel to the crowd, and after his message the new believers were baptized, and 3,000 people were added to the church! What a tremendous start in Christian missions!

The first three centuries of Christianity saw rapid expansion as the message went out wherever the Christians went. Think of the many who traveled home from Jerusalem after the Day of Pentecost. Names that stand out early in Acts are Peter, Stephen, and Philip. Later we read of the missionary trips of Paul and of Barnabas. The disciples probably left Jerusalem sooner than they had intended, for persecution drove them out. Tradition says that the Gospel was even taken to India by the Apostle Thomas.

The political climate of that day aided the spread of Christianity. The Roman Empire controlled vast areas that benefited from the empire's beautiful highway system and river tradeways. The common language was Greek, and this helped people crossing cultures. In this setting, and with the fervor of the early Christians who were even willing to die for their faith, Christianity spread rapidly in the first three centuries.

• Dimmed but not destroyed. But the light of the Gospel was dimmed in the period that followed. During Constantine's rule of the Roman Empire, Christianity became the official religion of the Empire (320-325). Theodosius I declared it the exclusive religion in A.D. 380. The church became so secure that it began to be involved in politics. It stressed the ceremonial, settled down in tradition and comfort, and lost its strong missionary zeal. However, we do owe gratitude to some in the monastic movement who continued missionary work.

One person who stands out in this period is St. Patrick, the great evangelist to Ireland. Many think of him as Irish, but he was born to Christian parents in Britain about A.D. 389.

Patrick first went to Ireland against his will; as a boy he was captured along the coast and taken as a slave on a pirate ship. He was sold to a tribal chief in Ireland and for years worked as a swineherd. Because of his love for God, he was called Holy Boy.

The story is told that one night he heard a voice in a dream saying, "Wake up, your ship is waiting for you!" He escaped and fled to the coast 200 miles away, and there he found a ship ready to sail! But traveling as a stowaway he nearly starved.

St. Patrick went a second time to Ireland, this time because he felt God wanted him to go. His family begged him not to return to the place where he had suffered such hardship. Later he wrote, "The only reason I had to return to the people I once escaped from was the Gospel and its promises." After 30 years in Ireland, Patrick had seen over 100,000 converted to Christ (J. W. Cowart, "The Story of Saint Patrick," *HIS,* InterVarsity, March 1980, pp. 1-5).

Because invasions by barbarians troubled most countries of Europe, Ireland became a haven for scholars. Kane in *A Global View of Christian Missions* says that the Irish monastic schools "kept the lamp of learning burning when the lights all over Europe were going out" (Baker, p. 37).

It was Boniface, an English nobleman and Benedictine monk, who took the Gospel to Germany. Many monasteries and seminaries were founded there. Through the centuries the Gospel continued to be carried to other parts of Europe so that by 1200 most of Europe was nominally Christian. The Gospel had already been taken to North Africa and Ethiopia in the early centuries. It had traveled through Asia Minor and Central Asia, to India and even to China. History tells us of the first missionary to China, a man named Alopen, who went there in A.D. 635.

During this same period of time, Christianity was threatened by a new religion. Islam had its beginnings in Arabia in 622. The Crusades of the twelfth and thirteenth centuries, when Christians moved out militarily against Islam, nearly destroyed the missionary vision of the church. Muslims still look back to the brutal tactics of the Christians of that day.

• Renewed Responsibility. Roman Catholic missions moved out in the fifteenth and sixteenth centuries, as they followed the expansion of Portugal and Spain into the New World. Then came the Protestant Reformation. We would expect that missions would have moved with zeal from Luther's emphasis on salvation by faith and the authority of the Scriptures. But surprisingly the new emphasis did not immediately affect missions.

It was a German movement known as Pietism that finally stirred up the missionary vision of the Protestant church. The father of this movement was Philip Spener (1635-1705). J. Herbert Kane says, "As the Protestant Reformation was the revolt against false doctrines and corrupt morals of the Church of Rome, so the Pietist movement was a revolt against the barren orthodoxy and dead formalism of the state churches of Protestant Europe."

Kane sums up the Pietistic view: "There can be no missionary vision without evangelical zeal; there can be no evangelical zeal without personal piety; there can be no personal piety without a genuine conversion experience" (*A Global View of Christian Missions,* pp. 76-77).

The Pietists founded Halle University, a cornerstone for missionary work, and the Danish Halle Mission, the first Protestant mission. A student at Halle, Count Zinzendorf, founded the Moravian Mission. Other continental societies followed, and some work began in North America.

But it is William Carey who stands out in history as the Father of Modern Missions. He stressed Christian responsibility to reach the lost. As this English cobbler prayed for the world, he sensed a new calling and obligation. In 1792, Carey published a pamphlet which some acclaim to be the most convincing missionary paper ever written—*An Enquiry into the Obligation of Christians to Use Means for the Conversion of the Heathens.*

Carey could have been discouraged by his staunch Calvinist colleagues who told him, "When God pleases to convert the heathen, He will do it without your aid or mine." But he was not distracted, and he formed the Particular Baptist Society for Propagating the Gospel Among the Heathen.

Carey met opposition from his family too. Nevertheless, in 1793 he sailed for India with his wife, four children, and two other companions. His journals reveal struggles through the next 40 years—serious financial problems, his wife's mental illness, prevalence of disease, and the destruction by fire of his precious manuscripts for translation. His commitment to "Attempt great things for God and expect great things from God" prevailed. Many heard the Gospel in India, and he translated Scripture into 35 languages and dialects (Mary Drewery, *William Carey,* Zondervan).

The Haystack Group is linked to the beginning of American missions. The place was Williams College, and the year was 1806 when an unusual band of young men, inspired by Carey, came together. They met regularly to pray for the world, usually under the trees. One day there was a sudden thunderstorm. They ran for shelter near a haystack and became known as the Haystack Group. Together they resolved to reach the world for Jesus Christ—"We can do it if we will!" (J.H. Kane, *Understanding Christian Missions,* Baker, p. 148)

Some of these men went on to Andover Seminary where they met Adoniram Judson who was also interested in missions. He was America's first foreign missionary, leaving for Burma in 1812, under the American Baptist Foreign Mission Society.

Other denominational mission boards were organized around this time in America. Some of these included the Methodist Episcopal (1819), the Protestant Episcopal (1821), the Presbyterian (1831), and the Evangelical Lutheran (1837).

• Expansion by Faith. But the beginning of the faith missions in the middle of the nineteenth century offered a new concept. Denominations were facing tremendous financial pressures and were finding it difficult to send missionaries.

It was James Hudson Taylor who led the way for faith missions. After one term working along the coast of China in the mid-1800s, he believed that God wanted him to work among the inland people where no missionary had gone. But the boards in England felt that they could not be committed to so great a task. As Taylor wrestled over this need, God seemed to speak to him: "Why not go yourself, and trust God to work through you?" But Taylor knew he must have others to go with him, the need was so great. He wanted to take 24 fellow workers with him. He had learned to trust God for himself, but to trust God for the care of others was a larger undertaking!

Taylor wrote that he was so burdened as he faced this intense inner conflict that others noticed his troubled spirit. A friend, Mr. Pearse, invited him to the seashore at Brighton for a rest. He attended church there, and wrote:

> On Sunday, June 25, 1865, unable to bear the sight of a congregation of a thousand or more Christian people rejoicing in their own security while millions were perishing for lack of knowledge, I wandered out on the sands alone, in great spiritual agony; and there the Lord conquered my unbelief, and I surrendered myself for this service. I told Him that all responsibility as to issues and consequences must rest with Him, that as His servant, it was mine to obey and follow Him—His, to direct, to care for, and to guide me and those who would labor with me" (Marshall Broomhall, *Hudson Taylor, The Man Who Believed God,* China Inland Mission, London, 1929, p. 117).

The entry for his journal on June 27 reads: "Went with Mr. Pearse to the London and County Bank, and opened an account for the China Inland Mission" (p. 22). It was the first appearance of the new name. The foundation of the China Inland Mission was laid as interdenominational, evangelical, and holding to the principle of faith at the center of its operation. Other faith missions followed in the latter part of the nineteenth century, in response to the need.

• Costly Commitment. The Great Century of Missions, the nineteenth century, saw the list of missionaries grow. Horace Underwood moved out to Korea, Verbeck to Japan, Livingstone and Moffat to Africa. It is impossible to name them all. Their vision of expansion was helped by colonization. The steam engine opened up the corners of the world. Missionaries built hospitals, schools, colleges, and orphanages.

As we read the history of this era, we are struck with the tremendous personal sacrifices made by the missionaries—lack of communication, years of isolation, physical deprivations, and threat of disease and death. Added to these was discouragement from rejection of the message. We are struck with the perseverance and faith of those who labored for years before they saw any fruit. Adoniram Judson spent 6 years in Burma before he saw any converts; for Robert Morrison in China, it was 7 years. The Primitive Methodists worked in Northern Rhodesia for 13 years before they baptized any African. But it was worse in Thailand. The American Congregational missionaries there withdrew after laboring for 18 years with no converts. The American Baptists withdrew after 17 years without response. The American Presbyterians saw their first convert in Thailand after 19 years (J.H. Kane, *Understanding Christian Missions,* p. 155).

The missionaries of the nineteenth century had to move out with a commitment that faced death as a real possibility. Michael Griffiths in *The Church and World Mission* comments,

> An earlier generation of missionaries never expected to return home, but was determined to do its utmost to preach Christ before being carried off by diseases for which there was little in the way either of prophylaxis or cure. ... They were mainly short-termers because they had no choice and died in the full flush of youth, while still seeking to understand language and culture (Zondervan, p. 13).

West Africa was referred to as "the white man's grave." Out of 35 missionaries who went to Ghana between 1835 and 1870, only two survived more than two years. Melville Cox went with the Methodists to Liberia in 1833. He died four months later, but his last words were, "Let a thousand fall before Africa be given up" (Kane, *Understanding Christian Missions,* p. 156). Today, the church in Africa is the fastest growing church in the world.

What heroes of faith! What costly commitment! No wonder the nineteenth century was called the Great Century of Missions!

## Missions in the Twentieth Century

The missions movement continued its momentum of global expansion on into the twentieth century. Now as this century moves toward the close, the new challenge—"A Church for Every People by the Year 2000"—becomes a feasible goal.

• All Systems Go. Although venture into space has become more common, we still recall with emotion man's first step on the moon. It was a beautiful Sunday evening in Liberia, with a tropical moon shining out over the Atlantic Ocean. Bob sat on the beach with a little transistor radio, and followed those tense moments as the lunar module descended three feet per second. Five—four—three—two—and as he looked up at the moon, sitting on the beach in Africa, he heard the words, "*Eagle* has landed." And a few hours later man stepped out onto the moon, "a giant step for mankind."

But long before that moment, the equipment was readied, the men—Armstrong, Aldrin, and Collins—were trained and in top shape, and at the time of the launch, the word was, "All systems are go."

The twentieth century can be characterized by "All Systems Are Go." It seems that everything has been readied for the final countdown, with trained personnel, specialized equipment, and the financial means to do the job in this century. Let's take a closer look.

This century has been marked with a phenomenal increase in the number of sending agencies. The faith mission movement has endured and expanded, and most of these missions operate in a businesslike manner. New and creative ideas in technology and teaching concepts have been used to help missions continue to move out in evangelism and church growth.

Student movements have been important in this century. The Student Volunteer Movement of the 1880s paved the way. In 50 years, spanning into this century, this movement sent over 20,000 to the mission field. Student organizations in this century have continued the global emphasis. Bible institutes and Christian colleges have increased in number, turning out more volunteers. The Scriptures have been put into many languages and dialects by Wycliffe Bible Translators and other missions.

• Breakdowns and Delays. But even with these encouraging movements, the twentieth century has not always been ideal for missions.

Most missions had to cut back during the Great Depression of the 1930s. One exception was the China Inland Mission which moved ahead by faith and sent over 200 missionaries to China!

After the Russian Revolution of 1917, Communism became a threat. In 1949 China was taken over by the Communists, and all missionaries were expelled from that great land. Gains in Communism have slowed the progress of mission activity in many countries.

More detrimental was a change in theological motivation in some sectors. "The Layman's Foreign Mission Enquiry of 1932," a study made of missions in the Orient, was part of the set-back. There were some good ideas that came from this study, but the conclusion was drawn that the aim of Christian missions should be cooperation with other religions—to see the best in them, rather than working toward conversions (Terry C. Hulbert, *World Missions Today*, ETTA, p. 29). The doctrine of neo-universalism crept into some churches, teaching that since Jesus Christ died for men everywhere, all men are saved already, even without knowledge of Jesus Christ. From that, the conclusion would be that there is no urgency to reach people for Christ.

Two world wars brought problems. Then came the wars in Korea and Vietnam. The struggles in the U.S. over Vietnam, the concerns for civil rights, the rioting, the student protests, and the change of lifestyles all seemed to dampen the outreach to others through missions.

"Missionary, Go Home!" was the cry in parts of the world in the early 1970s. With the rise of nationalism, a moratorium on sending missionaries began in Africa and moved to other parts of the world. Missions evaluated their work and their relationships with national churches. In many cases, after some time of tension, the move has been toward better relationships in cooperative efforts.

In recent years, the political unrest in many areas of the world, accompanied by acts of terrorism, has touched missions. Missionaries are often identified with the country of their citizenship and can be targets of revolutionary attack. Missions are dealing with hard questions in political situations where human rights are violated. For some, a new term—liberation theology—has entered the picture.

• Go-Ahead Given. But in spite of these problems, missions are moving ahead with unprecedented gains. When the world opened up after World War II, many new missions were formed.

We were in college in the late 1940s and early 1950s, and we noticed a number of men in our classes who had been in the service. They were preparing to go back into the world, this time with the Gospel. During our summers at Word of Life Camp in New York, we worked with returning servicemen who told us the needs of the world. As we gathered around the campfire and missionary speakers challenged us to "stand in the gap," it is little wonder that we were ready to look out to the world. We already knew those who were preparing to go to Africa, South America, Japan, New Guinea, or wherever the Lord might lead. The world had opened up after World War II, and countries welcomed American missionaries.

Then followed the years when many nations gained independence from colonial powers, bringing in a new era. The status of the national church changed too, and moved toward independence. The emerging Third World missions became part of the force. Through the years this arm has increased in strength.

The new prosperity of the middle class, especially in the U.S., supported budgets for missions. Programs and personnel expanded.

The 1960s were characterized by new ideas. The world grew even smaller with jet air travel and modern communications. The idea of the short term emerged. Then students went abroad just for the summer, and the summer missionary project was born.

After the student unrest of the 1960s settled down, young people seriously looked at global opportunities. The Urbana Missionary Conventions of the Inter-Varsity Christian Fellowship had a great influence in this, along with other student works such as Campus Crusade for Christ and The Navigators.

Modern equipment has streamlined mission operations. The students at the Urbana convention receive individualized computer printouts from InterCristo, matching them to potential job opportunities around the world with more than 250 agencies! Communication satellites remind us of other resources of modern technology yet to be tapped for missions.

An exciting turn of events came in the late 1970s with the opening of China to the outside world. Missions wait to hear more about the outreach to the one billion there.

• Twentieth-Century Countdown. Well into the 1980s, there is yet another look for missions. It really is not a new look, but one which reflects the original style. Mission agencies that have pioneered in taking the Gospel to new lands, that have helped start churches, and that have worked with the national churches in partnership, are looking even harder for the unreached peoples. And this brings us right back to the goal we mentioned earlier—the slogan we see often in mission literature today—A Church for Every People by the Year 2000.

As we look ahead to the rest of the century, what are some of the influences on missions we might anticipate? Certainly, inflation and economic turmoil will be major world problems. Missions will have to face the deep concerns of world hunger, global unrest, and the ever-widening gap between the haves and the have-nots. Missions will be affected by changes in the balance of power of leading nations.

There are so many questions we might ask. What will be the relationship between the church inside China and the church outside? How will new technology assist missions? How will the fervor of Muslim evangelism affect missions? What strides will be seen in the growth of Third World missions?

History has forced missions to set realistic goals, to set time limits, and to feel a sense of urgency to fulfill the Great

Commission in the final countdown of the twentieth century!
History helps us look at where we are and where we are going. And it reminds us that our God, the God of all times, the God of all nations who holds the hearts of the kings in His hand, is still at work through men and women carrying out His mission today. Have you found your place in God's mission program?

# 4

# The Next Step—
# Mission Strategy

"Good morning, I am Hero 1, the world's first educational robot." Bob couldn't believe his ears. He was at the Rotary Club in Stevensville, Michigan. The speaker was Hero 1, produced by Heath Company of nearby St. Joseph.

Bob said, "I watched with amazement as it traveled around the room. It asked that a light be turned down because it bothered its eyes." The chief engineer who had brought the robot to Rotary explained that it had the same senses as a human being. He pointed out the hand, the elbow, the eyes. Hero 1 had a computerized voice based on sound synthesis so it could be programmed to speak in any language of the world. Bob told us, "But when Hero 1 sang 'Happy Birthday' to one of the members, that was just too much!"

The engineer explained how the idea of Hero 1 had been conceived. The science of robotics is a new field with many industrial implications. But what interested Bob was the research, planning, and strategy that had gone into producing and marketing a tool with such potential.

Bob thought of the many people who had been involved in setting goals and standards. He thought of the marketing research. The need for such a teaching tool was carefully evaluated before the project was begun. He thought of the engineering triumphs, the design functions, and the thousands of hours of careful goal-setting and planning. This was strategy. The result is that for at least two years, this remarkable robot will be in full production for a market that is waiting.

## Need for Strategy

Any worthwhile endeavor involves strategy. Jesus gave us His strategy for missions. Let's look at the goal He set before us and the plans He outlined to reach the goal.

> Therefore go and make disciples of all nations, baptizing them in the name of the Father and of the Son and of the Holy Spirit, and teaching them to obey everything I have commanded you. And surely I will be with you always, to the very end of the age (Matt. 28:19-20).

• There it is: the goal is to *make disciples* of all nations. The goal is not just to be sure that everybody hears the Gospel once; He wants them to hear, to understand, to accept Him, and to become His disciples. Jesus even outlined how to do it. He said we must *go.* We must reach people where they are in their own culture. He says to *preach the Gospel* (Mark 16:15; Luke 24:47). To do this so that the hearers understand the Gospel, accept Christ, and are baptized as Christians is a process that will take time. Jesus also said to *teach* them to obey His commands, that they might follow Him and be His disciples. The result is a church that can *reproduce* itself around the world.

• In these verses, Jesus pointed to the *target area* to be reached, *all nations.* We often think of this as going from country to country; however, the biblical meaning of nations seems to be *cultural groups of people,* so we can really say *all peoples.* Missions find that it is good to work through people groups; they say this is a manageable approach. Edward R. Dayton in his book, *That Everyone May Hear,* gives a good definition of a people group:

A number of different things contribute to create a distinctive people group, one that in some way shares a common way of life, sees itself as a particular group having an affinity for one another, and differs to some extent from other groups of people. This may be because of shared language, religion, ethnicity, residence, occupation, class, caste, special situation, or some combinations of these (MARC, p. 58).

- Strategy usually includes a time reference as to when the goal is to be reached. Jesus said, "And surely I will be with you always, to the very end of the age" (Matt. 28:20). The time will come when the work is to be finished. We see recorded in Mark 13:10 when Jesus was telling His disciples about the signs of the end of the age, He said, "And the Gospel must first be preached to all nations."

Some missiologists are proposing a time reference for planning in missions, a time when every people might have a church in their own people group. A banner across the front of the auditorium at the 1980 World Consultation on Frontier Missions in Edinburgh, Scotland set the challenge: A Church for Every People by the Year 2000. This envisions a fellowship of Christians in each people group by the year 2000, capable of reaching out to others in their own culture.

It is estimated that the world's population will be between six and seven billion by the year 2000. Already we are behind— of the four billion people in the world, over two billion are not able to hear the Gospel through existing churches in their own group. Is it really possible to evangelize the world by the year 2000?

It has been suggested that it will take a special kind of strategy, closure strategy. According to Bradley A. Gill of the U.S. Center for World Missions,

Closure strategy says that it is not enough for us today to go across the world and do a good job. We must work toward finishing the task, toward bringing all the sheaves in, toward completing the full count of the bride of Christ" ("A Church for Every People," *Perspectives on the World Christian Movement*, eds. Ralph D. Winter and Steven C. Hawthorne, William Carey Library, p. 599).

• So now let's look to missions and see how they are coming along with their plans. Does it surprise you that they do have a strategy? Missions have not always been good at planning and setting goals, but one of the exciting things in the past few years of missions has been an emphasis on strategy. Someone has said that if you aim for nothing, you get nothing, and how true that is!

We were fortunate that we learned to use strategy in the building of a hospital. In establishing a medical practice, we had to set goals, maintain certain standards, and periodically make evaluations of success or failure. Of course, there was daily evaluation of the medical treatment of patients; but the development of the staff, the training of nationals to take over in key areas, the goal of having Christian Liberian physicians and administrators in the future—these were also measurable goals.

We felt that SIM encouraged the use of strategy. In the early 1970s, it was Bob's privilege to take a management training class, devised by the American Management Association, which helped strengthen his concept of strategy. Through the years we had to develop one-year plans for the hospital, five-year plans, and even some ten-year plans.

Gordon MacDonald, pastor of Grace Chapel in Lexington, Massachusetts, and an authority on world missions says, "A lack of strategy is frequently at the root of personnel dropouts, sloppy and subpar work, unusual degrees of conflict between field leaders, and field programs that are achieving little success" (Wade T. Coggins, *So That's What Missions Is All About,* Moody, p. 38). He goes on to say that failure to develop a statement of strategy leaves the home board, the director, the supporters and, most of all, the missionaries in doubt as to what they are doing.

When someone asks a Liberian how he's doing, the reply may be, "Oh, I'm trying small-small." That means he's not good, not bad, or maybe even there's small improvement. In other words, he's still hanging in there, though the going may be tough. Missions that don't have goals and plans really don't know how they're doing either. They're just "trying small-small."

## Barriers to Strategy

If strategy is so important in missions, why then have some missions been guilty of not taking goal-setting seriously?

• First of all, it's not always easy to make plans. People often lack confidence in determining the needs. Then too, there is a danger of contentment, the "we've-always-done-it-this-way" syndrome.

• A barrier of a different sort is sometimes called job satisfaction. The missionary may have brought a group of believers along the way to maturing in Christ and now it's difficult for him to set a goal of leaving the work with others, of turning it over to the national church. Because of the discomfort of changing methods, many people stay with the "status-quo" syndrome—"don't rock the boat."

• Busyness also gets in the way. The sowing aspect of ministry receives so much attention that the harvest is neglected. So often we were caught up in the hectic night-and-day call of the medical work in Liberia. But finally, as we were forced to sit down and prepare strategy plans for one year, for five years, and ten, we had to consider the goal of making disciples through the means of medicine and related ministries at ELWA. We saw the vision of the fruit and profited from it.

• Changes in personnel, which happen frequently on the field, can add confusion to making plans. Strong personalities too often influence the laying of plans, as people pursue their favorite projects.

• It may surprise you that one of the negative reactions to strategy is the feeling, "Strategy isn't spiritual. We'll just let God do the leading." Granted, the Holy Spirit does guide and sometimes in ways we have not anticipated; but He can direct in carefully laid plans too. We don't just sit and wait for whatever comes along.

When we were getting ready to go to Liberia the first time, we knew that we were going to build a hospital and that there was no equipment. So we took along everything given to us! Fortunately, the Lord did direct in all this so that the equipment needs were supplied. But we still have to smile at one offer from a medical supply firm—140 crutches, the old-fashioned unadjustable kind! Of course, we took them along! Most of them were too long for the average Liberian but from time to time we gave them out, or shared them with other hospitals, and some of them are still in the attic of the hospital! That was one item we didn't consider in our planning! We just let it happen!

## Facilitators of Strategy

So strategy is important. But who develops it? The answer is that it is developed in different areas of the work from the contributions and ideas of many people. But it is vitally important to have people with vision. There will always be those who have ten reasons why something can't work. It takes visionaries to come up with new and creative ideas, and missions need such people.

• One place where strategy is laid is at the headquarters of the mission, by the board or council which determines the overall direction of the work. Some missions give more authority to the homeland board than do others. Board members are in the position to look for the workers needed. They can communicate to the missionaries the general direction of the mission. They look for the finances needed. They keep the constituency informed, and communicate the direction of the mission to the sending churches.

• On the field, a field council or board gathers information from the workers and plans the strategy within the larger vision of the organization. In some missions, the field council has a stronger voice than the home board or even is the final authority. A statement as to where the final authority rests is essential.

The different divisions or ministries on the field should set their own objectives. It is also important for individual work-ers—both missionaries and nationals—to have a personal sense of direction through individual goals to be met. Confusion is avoided when people know just where they fit into the strategy.

• Another voice in missions comes from the national church. As the church becomes more mature, it works in partnership with the mission in planning. Then as it becomes independent, it moves on out to develop its own strateg*Bin reaching out in mission activity. We'll talk more about that later.

Mission-church relationships have not always been without tensions, but missions have learned much through these expe-riences. Sometimes political situations have forced missions to look at objectives with national workers more realistically than they would have otherwise. Dale Everswick of TEAM wrote in the mission magazine, *Horizons,* "TEAM in Zimbabwe has been liberated! We have been freed to start again, to retain what was good from the past, and to set new goals in a brand new country with wide open doors." He went on to tell of Zim-babwe's revolution which brought so many changes: "It has helped TEAM to change for the better. It has shaken us up. It has forced us to reevaluate our work. It has helped us to see ourselves as other people see us, because Zimbabweans today are much freer to speak their mind to a white person. What they say is refreshing if it isn't too painful!" (Vol. 58, No. 4, 1982, p. 3)

Through the years, we appreciated so much the counsel from our Liberian staff. Mrs. Priscilla Payne came to us just when the hospital was going to open, and she has been a part of the ELWA Hospital ever since, and for many of those years as director of nursing. She is the wife of Bishop Roland Payne, the head of the Lutheran Church in Liberia, and she brought with her much wisdom and concern for her people. She is the kind of person who can make suggestions to a doctor without him even knowing that she has. In her gracious way through the years, she helped to guide in plans—not only medically, for which we fondly called her "Dr. Payne"—but also in decisions for the welfare of the staff and in spiritual outreach. The voice of the national staff is of tremendous assistance.

## Process of Strategy

Workers together—the home boards, the field personnel (missionaries and nationals), the national churches, indigenous missions—building strategy together.

• Let's go behind the scenes in missions and look at how they go about it. First, they look for the people to be reached. A closer scrutiny will reveal that there are two orbits in missions. There is the orbit where churches have already been planted; where, while missionaries are still looking for new converts, there is the watering and tilling that goes on to build the church, to teach the disciples, that they might in turn reach others.

## THE EPICUREAN

SO I SAID, I WISH YOU MISSIONARIES WOULD PLEASE SHUT UP ABOUT <u>OTHER</u> PARTS OF THE WORLD. WHAT ABOUT <u>THESE</u> PARTS? WHAT ABOUT PEOPLE RIGHT HERE WHO DON'T LISTEN TO THE GOSPEL?

AND HE SAID, WHAT ABOUT PEOPLE OVER THERE WHO DON'T HAVE IT TO LISTEN TO?

SUDAN INTERIOR MISSION

Figure 2

The second orbit is harder to see, for it includes people who live in unreached areas where no viable church exists. They make up about 80 percent of the world's non-Christians. Researchers have identified over 16,000 such people groups having common sociological ties—sometimes pockets of people within other cultures and difficult to identify—but no church witness. Many of these groups are within the large blocs of Muslims, Buddhists, Hindus, or are scattered out in tribal areas. Large numbers are in China, Africa, India, and some are even in the inner cities of America! These are people who do not have ordinary means—such as a church—to bring the Gospel to them.

Ralph Winter, founder of the U.S. Center for World Mission, points out that the tragedy today is that most of our mission efforts are concentrated on those who are in the first orbit. Only about five percent of the work force of 55,000 Protestant missionaries today serves in the second orbit where the Gospel has not taken root. True, it is not easy to go to these unreached peoples. In fact, it may seem next to impossible to go through usual means to reach some groups. However, missions are trying hard to find creative ways to reach them. The people-by-people approach seems to be less of an impossible task than person-by-person.

• Have you wondered where missions go for all the information they need to enter a new area? Research is important, and today there are agencies that specialize in researching and analyzing information for missions. Some of these agencies are Missions Advanced Research and Communication Center (MARC—a ministry of World Vision International); the U.S. Center for World Mission; and the Lausanne Strategy Working Group, an outgrowth of the International Congress on World Evangelization in Switzerland in 1974. The *World Christian Encyclopedia*, published by Oxford University Press, gives much information. *Operation World*, a book prepared for world intercession by P. J. Johnstone (Send the Light Publications) also provides a wealth of information, country by country. Mission agencies are developing their own research departments and are sharing information with one another.

• Surveys are made into new areas under consideration. We have been impressed by the ability of corporations to come into a Third World country and develop resources where it would seem that odds are against them. This can happen because they have carefully surveyed the situation. When we arrived in Liberia, we drove through Firestone Plantation on our way to ELWA. The row after row of rubber trees, the thousands of workmen, the large market area, the housing, all confirmed that surveys had led them to believe that rubber would grow well in Liberia.

Along the border of Guinea, in the cooler and refreshing climate of the Nimba Mountains, is a beautiful little town cut right out of the mountains, planned by Swedish architects for LAMCO, an iron ore mining company. This is a cooperative venture by Liberian, American, and Swedish companies. The homes are cool and comfortable, and the town has an olympic-sized pool, tennis courts, and even a golf course. When we vacationed in that area, we would watch the huge trucks winding through the mountain to bring out the iron ore. But before LAMCO had all this, they had to carefully survey the area to determine the feasibility for such an operation. They brought in geologists to make sure there was ore to be mined, before they built a railroad and a town.

Missions too survey new areas. They talk to other missions, to embassies, to anyone who can give information. If they are entering a country where they haven't worked, they find out if the government will welcome their presence. They look into the climate, the geography, the roads. Anthropologists and sociologists can give light on the people and their customs. The history of a country is important. Missions want to know the population distribution and growth. Linguists help with questions about the languages. The economy of the area needs to be appraised to understand what kinds of programs the people will be able to maintain without outside aid.

Other possible questions are: What are the prevalent diseases? Is some other mission task force already reaching these people? Does that group need assistance?

• Target locations are picked. Sometimes these are in large areas where the mission already works, but focusing on a new people. For instance, in the early 1900s, workers from India were brought to Kenya by the British to help build a railroad. After the completion of their work, they stayed on. This grow-ing population has long been neglected by missions. A tight-knit group, they are mostly merchants. Recently, the Africa Inland Mission and the International Mission together estab-lished a witness to this Asian community in Kenya.

Frequently, after years of working only in rural regions, a mission will select certain cities as new target areas. Many cultures are represented and often forgotten in crowded cities. It is predicted that by the year 2000, half of the world's popula-tion will live in cities.

• Missions look carefully at the people to assess their needs. They ask: What religion is practiced among the people? Is there any awareness of Christianity? Are there any key Christians? Are there any churches? Is there open opposi-tion to the preaching of the Gospel? Would new believers face persecution?

How receptive do the people seem to be? Will the Gospel seed fall on good soil? Is it the right time?

Certainly, missions want to concentrate where people are ready to hear. Some strategists feel it is a waste of time to labor long over unresponsive segments of people.

On the other hand, it has been the experience of missions that a people may appear to be resistant for years before there is a breakthrough. Pete and Sadie Ackley joined us in Liberia right before the opening of ELWA Hospital. After 16 years as bush missionaries in the Sudan, they had to leave along with other missionaries because of the civil war there. Pete and Sadie were God's choice to help at the ELWA Hospital to get things started. Everyone loved them for they were "people" missionaries; and while they worked in administration, they still would help out any place where needed.

Now they are back again in the Sudan. Recently Pete had the

privilege of baptizing fifteen young Mabaans in the Nile River. The Ackleys reminded us that SIM began work in southern Sudan among the Mabaans in 1930, when the people were like the land they lived on—isolated and unyielding. Three SIM missionaries were buried there, and more than 50 worked there from 1939 to 1964. When they had to leave at the time of the civil war, they could count on two hands the number of believers.

Sadie wrote, "Last year when we returned to the Sudan, we feared what we might find. To our utter amazement, we are seeing the long-awaited harvest. The same day when Pete baptized the fifteen Mabaans, there were 253 Udaks in two other areas who followed the Lord in baptism."

There is also a look at the physical and educational needs of the people. Sometimes it is very difficult to even begin to tell people of the Gospel if their physical needs are too great. Should help be given first?

• In planning strategy, an understanding of the culture of the group is mandatory to presenting the Gospel in a way they can perceive. *Contextualization* is the term used now in missions. This means that the Gospel is presented in a way that is understandable in the context of their culture—their behavior, values, beliefs, and world view. Missiologists say that much time is lost, confusion stirred up, and unreached people offended, because missionaries fail to understand the culture or through it see an opening to present the Gospel.

Remember how Paul spoke to the people of Athens as they gathered on Mars Hill? He saw an opening in their religion and his message was:

Men of Athens! I see that in every way you are very religious. For as I walked around and observed your objects of worship, I even found an altar with this inscription: TO AN UNKNOWN GOD. Now what you worship as something unknown I am going to proclaim to you (Acts 17:22-23).

Recently we met someone who made use of his knowledge

of a culture right in our own backyard of Berrien County, Michigan. Every summer a special people group comes here by the hundreds, for this is one of the largest fruit-producing areas in the United States. Most of these migrant workers are Spanish Americans, and many of us would have difficulty communicating with them. They do not attend church since they usually are working seven days a week. In the past we inquired about ministries to them, but only recently have we met someone who has a unique evangelical witness to them.

Fernando, a young man from Argentina, is in Michigan to attend Grand Rapids School of the Bible and Music. He is taking the aviation course and plans to return to South America to fly for missions. For the past three summers, he has been a missionary to Berrien County as he heads up a witness to the migrant workers in a mission project of the Christian Reformed Church.

Fernando found a good way to get to know the people, to be accepted by them. Do you know one thing these Spanish Americans really appreciate as they have come north? Tortillas—the Mexican food they love! Two or three times a week Fernando gets into his little old car and drives the ninety miles to Chicago to pick up boxes and boxes of fresh tortillas! He buys these not to make money but to make friends with these people. As he makes the rounds from camp to camp with tortillas, he visits with the workers in their Spanish language and gets to know them. They really welcome him. He is one of them. Then as he invites them to his Bible studies or film showings, they know for sure that he is interested in them and their needs.

• After research has given the information needed, then there is the careful scrutiny of resources available. What methods would be best? What are the personnel needs? We'll talk about these later.

What about the financial resources? That's tough question that has to be asked. In this day of economic depression around the world, when the prices of supposedly stable commodities such as oil, iron, rubber, and other raw materials fluctuate so much, it is very important to consider the cost. Missions do not want projects to become monkeys on their backs. They should not undertake programs that will be liabilities to the national church.

Missions also ask: Is there another way to do the job? Would it be better to cooperate with someone else in this venture? Should we pool our resources? Missions are cooperating with one another to get the job done.

• Next, priorities are set. What is urgent? What are long-term needs? Long-range planning looks five or ten years down the road.

• Finally, when the plans are in motion, periodic evaluation is a must in carrying out the strategy. If the goal is not reached, what is the reason? Should changes be made in methods? Or personnel? Or is the time just not right? Missions must continue to check the progress in fulfilling the Great Commission.

In *Stop the World, I Want to Get On,* C. Peter Wagner, former missionary and professor of church growth, says,

> In a way I hate to say it, but it is sadly true that the mission fields of the world are overloaded with evangelistic programs that are not functioning properly. Sadder yet, many people deeply involved in them don't even realize the fact. . . . In many of these programs, believe it or not, the results are not even tested (William Carey Library, p. 95).

Wagner reminds us that missionaries should not settle comfortably into a program without examining what is being done in terms of results. Evaluation of strategy with a willingness to change plans is essential for progress.

We've stepped behind the scenes in missions, and we've seen how important strategy is with planning, careful use of resources, setting of priorities, and evaluations. Does it sound like it falls together neatly? It doesn't always work that way! But strategy is important! Prayer paves the way and is a part of every step taken. But behind the most carefully laid plans is the element of surprise and yet expectation, for God may bring changes. And there is a realization that only He can bring the increase.

Just strategy is not enough, but it does help. When strategy is combined with prayer and the work of God's Holy Spirit, fruit will be harvested. Strategies can change, but the goal does not change. The goal: Not robots like Hero 1, but living disciples of Jesus Christ.

# 5

# Qualified Personnel Needed

On the plane enroute from North America, the new recruit opened the sealed envelope and read instructions for his mission abroad.

Dear Colleague,
As you become part of the task force building Christ's church worldwide, I want to share with you several personal matters that can make a great difference in your new life. Within a very short time after arrival, you will long for more training in Bible, communications, cultural understanding, political awareness, psychological insights, and for a deeper walk with God. You will feel that your own abilities do not match the demands before you and you will be right.

This is the opening paragraph of a letter that Charles Troutman, a retired missionary with the Latin America Mission, says he would like to put into the hands of every missionary leaving North America for the first time, to help prepare him for what he will face ("Steps to Mature Servanthood Overseas," *Evangelical Missions Quarterly,* January 1983, p. 26).

Personnel dispatched to go into another culture to carry the Good News are called missionaries. They need special qualifications, as Troutman suggests. They never seem to be overqualified.

Occasionally we hear someone say that all Christians are missionaries. What they probably really mean is that all Christians are to be witnesses of Jesus Christ. We would agree with that. However, for our use of the word *missionary,* we are going to limit it to those who go into another culture or another geographical area with the Gospel to make disciples. The word *missionary* originally came from the Latin word *mitto,* meaning "to send," as does the Greek word *apostello.* In Romans 10:14-15, we read Paul's questions: "And how can they hear without someone preaching to them? And how can they preach unless they are sent?"

What is your image of a missionary? It's hard to generalize because missionaries come in many varieties from as many different backgrounds. Some are neat and very organized. Some are easygoing and unaware of time. Many are individualists, nonconformists. But there's a family relationship among missionaries—even those from different missions—a "we're in this together" feeling. The longer missionaries are on the mission field, the more they feel part of a bicultural group. They are most at home with others who work overseas.

As a doctor at a mission hospital, Bob saw many missionaries from Liberia and from missions in other countries, as they came to the coast for medical care. Bob often asked, "How did you happen to come to Africa?" They shared something in common, a sense of God's direction in their lives which brought them to Africa.

One account we will never forget was from a member of our own staff. From 1962 to 1965, we saw God miraculously provide equipment and staff for the ELWA hospital, even sending us a dentist, a staff need that had not been listed yet! Dr. Suhail Zarifa was originally from the Gaza Strip between Israel and Egypt. He had gone to Egypt for his university and dental training. In Alexandria he heard shortwave broadcasts from ELWA and was fascinated by the Bible messages. On a visit back to the Gaza Strip, he met with a missionary who led him to put his faith in Jesus Christ.

After graduation, Suhail went back home to work as a dentist. He found himself concerned for the Arab people who did not know Jesus Christ. The opportunity came for Suhail and his older brother Saad to go to Canada, Suhail to attend Bible college and Saad to work as an engineer.

They had to find a place to stay, and it was the home of a former SIM missionary that was opened to them. She talked to them about ELWA, the very radio station from which Suhail had heard the Gospel! He learned of the need for an Arabic broadcaster, and the doors continued to open for him to join us there.

Most missionaries do not have such unusual circumstances to relate, but each story is unique in God's leading. We often hear it referred to as the *call* to be a missionary.

## But What in the World Is a Call?

A lot of people get hung up on the word *call*. Let's first look at some of the faulty ideas. The SIM cartoon (figure 3) helped us shoot down the idea that it has to be a vision, an audible voice from heaven, or even a bolt of lightning. We appreciate the last frame! "But the call is God's revelation to you of His will that all men hear the Gospel. So, maybe you should stop worrying about the call and start working on the answer."

To work on the answer involves walking in the will of God as a Christian, step by step, as He leads. That means knowing Jesus Christ as Lord and Saviour and desiring to do His will. It means understanding that it is God's will that all men hear the Gospel. It means realizing that each Christian is to be involved in carrying out God's mission to reach the world. And it means asking, "Lord, where do You want me to fit in?" This leads to a careful appraisal of your gifts and where they can be used. The counsel of others is very important in determining this.

Some people call it *guidance* rather than a *call*. A Christian seeking God's guidance as to how he fits into God's plan needs to know that missionary service is one option to be considered.

When questioned about the necessity of a call, Dr. Ian Hay, General Director of SIM International, responded,

Figure 3

In deciding on location, it's obvious that God isn't sending every believer to another country to serve ... but before a person assumes that he is to work at home, he should consider all the options open to him ... and the Scriptures make it very plain that the *whole* world must hear the Gospel. In the light of Christ's command, and the condition of the world, foreign missions is certainly a major option to consider ("No Voice from Heaven," *Africa Now,* SIM, November-December 1979, p. 2).

In times past, going to faraway places often meant hardship and death. Today people so easily travel around the world, for pleasure and business, that it certainly is not an unusual option to consider.

## THE EPICUREAN

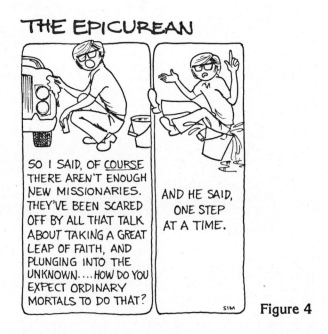

Figure 4

Finally, there's that step of faith which says, "I'll go if it's Your will," and then the continued following of His leading.

This is where doors open and close, even to the very last minute before leaving for the mission field. An open door is taken as God's leading, a sign of His approval. And there is a sure sense of direction.

We told you how we were challenged to consider missions during our college years. We were married the summer before Bob went to medical school, and we continued to pray about mission service while he was in medical school. Bob says you'll promise God anything during those first years of medical school! But during his surgery residency in Michigan, we still didn't know where we might serve. Then one night an SIM doctor and his wife, Dick and Marge Scheel, stopped by to show us pictures of their work. As they left, they mentioned that there was a need for a doctor in Liberia.

That rang a bell! We had followed with interest the beginning of radio station ELWA in Liberia. Just ten years earlier, Bob had succeeded Dick Reed in the Word of Life Hour Quartet when Dick went to be one of the founders of ELWA. Marian had stood on the dock to wave good-bye to Dick and Jane as they left New York harbor for Liberia in 1952. We had often thought of the combination of radio and medical missions. So Marian asked Bob, "Why don't you write Dick and find out if there is a need for a doctor at ELWA?"

Three weeks later, Marian again nudged him, "Why don't you just write and ask?" And so he did, and to our small faith and great surprise, Dick Reed wrote back that they had been praying for a doctor and a hospital for three years. Our letter arrived right before an important field council meeting, and armed with our letter, the needed hospital was approved!

The doors kept opening. We were accepted by SIM. The last door to be opened—clearance from a child neurologist in New York City to take Bobby to Africa, since he had suffered problems due to a severe reaction to his smallpox vaccination at eight months of age.

The call—responding to information received, acting responsibly to find out just where God wants us to be—and then walking with a sure sense of His direction. Guidance—trusting God even to the last minute.

## What Does a Missionary Look Like?

If you were sitting on a mission board looking at candidates, what physical traits would you look for? As a doctor, Bob was interested in the medical reports that came along to the field with new missionaries. However, he realized that there are few health problems that would keep a person from serving some-place in the world. Obviously, if a person has diabetes and needs frequent blood sugar evaluations, he won't be sent far into the interior where there are no medical facilities. Doctors do look to see if there are any disorders which would be difficult to handle in particular places. They look for medical signals that a person might have trouble working under tension. Health evaluations continue throughout the career.

Emotional stability is also an important part of the health picture. It's usually not the big problems that cause troubles on the field, but the hundred and one little irritations that eat away at the health of the missionary. For example, we blamed a lot on the heat and humidity in Liberia, where it stayed around 100 percent humidity all the time! This stirred up irrita-bility, causing flare-ups. Then there's pressure from the con-stant shortage of help and overlapping of job assignments. There are many situations that call for emotional stability. Women are often asked to do a man's job in a man's culture.

What would be some trouble signs in prospective candi-dates? Mission boards watch for people who are too introspec-tive, who have difficulty in sharing feelings. They look for those who fly off the handle too easily. They want to see feelings of self-worth in a candidate. They look out for the workaholic, someone who can never relax, and for the perfec-tionist who expects too much of himself and those around him. Psychological testing can show areas of concern and many times people can be helped.

## Why Do They Act That Way?

What are some other missionary qualifications? Let's look at the personality—or attitudinal—traits. These are the charac-teristics that can either rub the wrong way or mean smooth sailing and effective service. Our personalities show up in our actions.

• First, there must be *acceptance of self*. One African, speaking of the missionary who will succeed, said that he must project himself as an *individual* and not just as a foreign missionary. This is hard to do if a person has a low self-image. The missionary has to realize that God loves him as he is.

The missionary can be just as troubled with the success syndrome as anyone else, and there is the temptation to equate self-esteem with personal ideas of success. The missionary knows he is put on a pedestal by his home church, when in actuality he finds himself plugging away with no exciting statistics to report. If he is having a hard time feeling accepted by nationals and is struggling with his identity with other missionaries, it can be a long slide down from the pedestal! It is important for the missionary to accept himself and to realize that God is still at work in his life.

That doesn't mean that the missionary won't work on personal growth. In fact, it's good if he realizes that he is important enough to do just that! And there are certainly all kinds of opportunities for growth, especially as he is often stretched to work in areas for which he has no particular training. He is truly in "continuing education" as he works with new people, different cultures, and constant change.

• If a missionary can accept himself, it's easier for him to *accept others*. Because people come first in missions, this is a must.

You may wonder, "Can missionaries have an attitude of superiority?"

Yes, we can! It comes out in subtle ways. Perhaps it's that we just don't think "they" can ever come up to "our" standards—that old we/they syndrome. There's a fine line between having high standards and yet accepting those who in the struggle of growth have not attained that level. This acceptance is easier when we admit that we have not yet attained in many areas either.

Acceptance includes a genuine appreciation of other

cultures. People can hardly be separated from their culture. The missionary's attitude of acceptance continues on out into the marketplace, on the crowded money bus, or waiting in long lines for hours at a government bureau.

Acceptance of others and their ideas is all the harder if the missionary feels he has superior ideas, better technology, more money, and that he should take over. He may find that fellow workers from other countries are not always so impressed with his ideas. It is even more humbling to find out that some of their ideas can work better than his. We have observed that North Americans have a particularly hard time balancing their aggressiveness and energy.

Because of the need for teamwork in missions, acceptance of others shows up in important interpersonal relationships. Bob and a younger British doctor, Dr. John Cowan, had a good working relationship in Liberia. As partners, they had to accept one another with their differences. Bob was more outgoing, with a deep bass voice that could be heard around the hospital—sometimes a big advantage! Dr. John called him "The Voice Under Every Palm Tree," the title of a book about pre-tuned radios that ELWA distributed to people all over Africa. When Dr. Bob was under pressure, he tended to get even louder! Then Dr. John would say in a very British tone, "Now, Robert, you're getting quite brash!"

When Dr. John was under pressure, he tended to move more slowly. Then Dr. Bob would come behind him and jokingly spur him on with, "Now come on, John, stop being British and let's get moving!"

They developed a very good relationship because they accepted each other and their differences, and learned from one another.

It is sometimes easier for missionaries to accept those they feel they can help the most, those who are poorer or not as educated. They may not feel as comfortable around those who are of equal educational status or above.

One of the best pieces of advice we received when we went to Liberia came from older missionaries. They said it would be good for us to develop trusted friendships with those with whom we shared a lot in common. When we arrived, a Liberian surgeon and his wife had just returned from training in the United States and were setting up a medical practice in the capital city, Monrovia. He was one of the few Liberian doctors at that time. We got to know this couple, Nehemiah and Izetta Cooper, soon after our arrival, and through the years we have appreciated their friendship.

• *Sensitivity to others* is another essential trait. We heard a powerful illustration of this from Dr. Paul Brand, Professor of Surgery at Louisiana State University Medical School and Chief of Rehabilitation at the U.S. Public Health Service Hospital for leprosy patients at Carville, Louisiana. Dr. Brand is a world famous leprologist and a renowned hand surgeon. One of his first patients at Carville was Ambrose, a young, muscular French American. When Dr. Brand entered the examining room, he offered his hand to Ambrose. Dr. Brand thought by shaking hands he would show the patient that he was not afraid of the disease of leprosy and that he wanted to help him.

But Ambrose withdrew his hand and refused to shake hands with the doctor. Surprised by this seeming act of rejection, Dr. Brand asked him why he would not shake his hand. Ambrose replied that he never shakes hands with anyone. He went on to explain that due to the loss of sensory touch and perception from the disease, when he did shake hands he would invariably see the other person wince. He caused pain as he was not sensitive to the power of his muscular handshake.

Dr. Brand went on to challenge us, "How many times do we as missionaries extend the hand of the Gospel of Jesus Christ to those in need—a suffering world—but with a lack of sensitivity to their feelings, their needs, their attitudes, so that the very people we are trying to reach wince with pain?" There needs to be a graciousness, a sensitivity to others, as we offer help in Jesus' name.

• We recently saw an ad for a missionary mechanic needed by the Slavic Gospel Association to work in Europe. It read—"Must exhibit a spirit of servanthood and flexibility." A personality trait that is needed by missionaries is *adaptability.* A big danger signal is rigidity. Of course, certain jobs will always require exactness of performance. And many mission- aries by nature are very independent. With different tempera- ments working closely together there can be serious problems if each one insists on doing things his own way. There has to be teamwork.

• Blessed is the missionary who has the *ability to enjoy life.* There are holidays and traditions to be kept in a new culture. There are dignitaries to meet, government functions to attend. Can the missionary graciously accept the hospitality that is often so freely offered and really enjoy it?

We saw this in Bill and Betty Thompson at ELWA. They enjoyed their life in Liberia. Bill even enjoyed crocodile hunting at night—he'd have to enjoy it to want to look for those eyes that reflect from the flashlights as the boat goes down the river. Their ministry was all the more effective because they entered into the experiences of the people of Liberia.

• Part of enjoying life is a *sense of humor,* something no missionary should be without! Volumes could be written about missionaries in life's most embarrassing situations. It's certain- ly more fun to laugh at oneself than to cry.

We remember when it was our privilege to be invited to the executive mansion in Liberia for a private dinner given by then President William V.S. Tubman and Mrs. Tubman, honoring Ray de la Haye, former general manager of ELWA, and his wife, Sophie. On our way to the mansion, we stopped with Ray and Sophie to see another friend. Coming down the stairs of the two-story home, Bob tripped and fell flat on his face, ripping a hole in the knee of his suit! There was no time to change because we were due at the mansion. So in the car we applied Band-aids inside the pant leg of his navy pinstripe suit. We had a lot of fun joking with the others about this, and even with the dignified President Tubman, diffusing a potentially embarrass- ing situation. It helps to have a sense of humor and especially to be able to laugh at yourself.

• Another helpful trait is the *ability to hang in there,* with a vision of the work to be accomplished, and then to see it to the end. Blessed is the missionary who is not easily discouraged.

Have you met anyone who has all these good characteristics? Probably not. We haven't either. But to be effective, a missionary should be working on these important personality traits.

## What Does a Missionary Carry?

Besides his Bible and the message of the Gospel, the missionary today often is expected to take along other equipment. The late Byang Kato of Nigeria, past general secretary of the Association of Evangelicals of Africa and Madagascar, said, "The day when just anything will do is past. Spirituality is no substitute for ignorance. A missionary should be in possession of knowledge that can contribute to the progress of the country" ("African Outlines 'New Missionary' Qualifications," *Africa Now,* SIM, March-April 1971, p. 10).

This requires academic preparation. Mission requirements will vary according to the job to be done. A seminary degree is often required; most missions want at least a college education for career work. Special skills are taken along to help reach the whole person. A Liberian friend in government told us, "When a missionary applies for a visa, immigration officials look at what he or she can do to benefit the people of the country."

It is to be hoped that the career missionary also will bring prior work experience in his field. Many missions require this.

## The Most Essential Equipment

It could be easy to assume that a missionary is a spiritual giant. We tread softly as we talk about spiritual qualifications, for certainly in this area no missionary feels he has ever arrived. But the qualifications are high, for the missionary is an ambassador. Paul said, "And he has committed to us the message of reconciliation. We are therefore Christ's ambassadors, as though God were making His appeal through us. We implore you on Christ's behalf: be reconciled to God" (2 Cor. 5:19-20).

• The missionary is a genuine Christian, trusting Jesus Christ as his Lord and Saviour. The missionary is *a responsible and growing Christian,* continuing to rely on the power of God in his life and to walk with a sense of direction.

A good knowledge of the Word of God is a basic piece of equipment. There are biblical principles to pass on to others, no matter what the job is on the field.

The missionary needs up-to-date communication with God through his devotional life. This is a difficult thing to maintain, for busy schedules and interruptions can crowd out time with God unless the missionary is insistent on maintaining it. He needs to look for ways he can be fed spiritually by others.

• We've talked about personality traits that help with interpersonal relationships, but now we are going deeper into qualities that can be produced only by the power of God. Following the example of Jesus Christ, there must be *identification with others.* It's "being at home with the people." It's trying to do this even though you know you will never fully succeed, that you will still be a foreigner.

Two little Liberian boys lived with us one year in Michigan. Stanley was ten and Brucie was only five years of age. We were like the TV program, "Different Strokes"! They got along just beautifully. Their schoolteachers couldn't get over what well-adjusted children they were, and they brought home terrific report cards. The only problem—we couldn't claim credit for that! They have wonderful parents!

Brucie was in the first grade and at the age when he really needed a mother. So Marian tried hard to fill the slot that year, and she and Brucie grew really close. One day Marian goofed up on something that she knew his mother would do so much better, and she said to Brucie, "Oh, I'm so sorry, I'm really not a very good mother, am I?"

And he looked up at her so sympathetically and said, "O Aunt Marian, you're just fine. The only trouble, you're not black!" And somehow Marian knew she would never quite make it!

Try as hard as we can to identify with the people, we

missionaries will never completely make it; but it is certainly worth the effort to make progress toward it.

Like the missionary Paul, the effort to identify with the people is made with the help of Christ. Paul said,

> To the Jews I became like a Jew, to win the Jews. To those under the law I became like one under the law ... to those not having the law I became like one not having the law ... to the weak I became weak ... I have become all things to all men so that by all possible means I might save some. I do all this for the sake of the Gospel, that I may share in its blessings (1 Cor. 9:20-23).

There should be no prejudice in the heart of the missionary. Prejudice is a spiritual problem, and most missionaries would deny they have this problem. But Kane in *The Making of a Missionary* says, "The real test of a missionary's love for the people will show in the friends with whom he shares his leisure time" (Baker, p. 67). Missionaries work with nationals, but what about after work, when it's time to relax? Is the time always spent with fellow missionaries, fellow Americans or Europeans?

• The *servant attitude* is another spiritual characteristic which is patterned after Christ. Pride has to be dealt with and put aside. One national said, "We need missionaries as partners, not bosses." The attitude of servanthood is so important. Other people must come first.

The missionary's lifestyle is usually more simple than it would be in his homeland. But by comparison to the people to whom he ministers, he may appear wealthy. Don Hillis of TEAM commented on this: "Don't let your possessions possess you, but let people know that your house, jeep, projector, and other goods belong to you for their benefit" ("Honey, Locusts, & Hairy Garments," *Wherever*, TEAM, Fall 1981, p. 5).

It is the heart of love that puts it all together for the missionary. On the field we sometimes have heard it said about a missionary, "He loves our souls, but he doesn't love us." Nationals can look through to the heart.

Paul wrote, "We loved you so much that we were delighted to share with you not only the Gospel of God but our lives as well" (1 Thes. 2:8). A sharing of ourselves that is from the heart is the kind of love people can feel.

## Will the Real Missionary Please Stand Up?

Did you ever watch the TV program, "To Tell the Truth," and try to guess who was for real? After looking at the many qualifications of a missionary, you may wonder if there are any real missionaries.

The truth is that missionaries—like all other Christians—are very human. We have not seen the perfect missionary yet. Probably one of the best pieces of advice we ever received before going to Liberia was in candidate school. A mission leader said, "When you think of the mission, just think of your own church." Now maybe your church doesn't have any problems, but lots of churches do! There are many different personalities within a church, just like on the mission field.

You will recall Charles Troutman's words in his open letter to missionaries, "You will feel that your own abilities do not match the demands before you and you will be right." But we have a lot of respect for those who do continue to work on their equipment in order to be "thoroughly equipped for every good work" (2 Tim. 3:17).

Early in their missionary career Greg and Jean Giles wrote home:

> Strange as it may seem, after a year in Liberia we still don't feel like missionaries. Maybe this is because we have grown up with years of the "missionary myth." We don't wear pith helmets. We don't live in a mud hut. We don't even sleep under mosquito nets. And we have yet to fight off a wild elephant while trekking through the jungle.
>
> Instead, we live in an apartment in the capital city and fight traffic jams on our way to teach high school students.
>
> Perhaps we don't feel like missionaries because we realize that we don't fit the image of spiritual giants. Crossing the ocean didn't complete our sanctification. We still struggle with laxness

in prayer and personal devotions. We still leave undone the things we ought to have done, and do the things we shouldn't. In other words, we're much the same Christians here as we were back home ("Well Worth the Effort," *Africa Now,* SIM, November-December 1979, p. 7).

We like that kind of honesty, don't you? It reminds us to pray for missionaries who are just like the Christians back home.

# 6

# New on the Job?

"Welcome to the team! This life of faith is terrific!" We read the words again—"This life of faith is terrific!"

In 1962, as Bob was finishing his surgery residency, we had written to ELWA in Liberia. We knew we were going to be in on the building of a hospital and we thought we had some good questions.

We asked the General Manager of ELWA, Ray de la Haye, "Are there any funds for the building of the hospital?"

Ray replied, "No, but if this is God's will, then He has promised that He 'will meet all your needs according to His glorious riches in Christ Jesus' " (Phil. 4:19).

We asked, "Do you have any equipment?"

And he answered, "Only a used operating room light donated by Park Street Church in Boston, and an old operating room table (which when we finally unpacked it, proved to be an old delivery table). We believe this is the earnest of what is to come."

We asked, "What about staff?"

Ray wrote, "We have five nurses. One single nurse takes care of the missionary health, and the others, wives of radio staff, have started the clinic. They find the needs overwhelming."

And that's when he said, "Welcome to the team! This life of faith is terrific!"

This was a new experience for us. True, both of us had accepted Christ as Saviour, but it was something else to trust Him for such tremendous needs. But armed with encouragement from the de la Hayes, we took that leap of faith.

One reason we listened to Ray and Sophie de la Haye was that we knew they had years of experience and that their word was credible. They had served in West Africa since 1937, working among Muslims and establishing a Bible school. Three of their four living children were born in Africa. They had worked in Nigeria on the Hausa Bible Revision Committee. In 1954 Ray had been appointed director of SIM's radio station ELWA. Their work had been varied. They were what we call career missionaries.

Later they returned to the States to become representatives for ELWA. During their retirement, Sophie is a free-lance writer (she authored the missionary biography, *Tread upon the Lion*), and Ray has had other mission assignments from their retirement home in Florida.

There are various types of missionaries—career, short-termers, and tentmakers. First, let's look more closely at career and short-term missionaries.

## Career and Short-Term Missionaries

The mission task force is made up of a majority who are career missionaries, those who commit themselves to years of service. They bring a continuity to the work that is very important.

The career missionary is essential in such ministries as church planting that take time and require consistency. The model of a family living among the people is helpful. Career missionaries need to learn the language and gain a good understanding of the people and the culture.

The career person should be willing to move on as needed into different areas of the mission work. He may work himself out of a job in one place and move on to the next assignment.

He has been trained to be a missionary. Missions count on career people as the backbone of the work.

But with the ease of travel and the shrinking world perspective, short-term workers have entered the task force in growing numbers. Short-term assignments can range from a few weeks to a few years. This is a way many young people can go. On the other end of the spectrum, retired individuals can go, for they still have much to offer. And for the in-between ages, there are plenty of job opportunities. Relatives—often parents of missionaries—are put to work through short-term assignments while visiting loved ones.

In the right place at the right time, short-termers are a tremendous asset. Those with special skills can do a particular job. Sometimes it means filling in for a furloughing missionary. Sometimes it's to help out in a program that is short-term in itself, such as a construction project or disaster relief work. With nationalization in missions, short-termers fit in because their goals are short-range. They help alongside career missionaries who are overworked, easing the pressure for a time.

Recently we talked to a young woman trained to give technological assistance in setting up X-ray machines. She is donating three months of her time to travel through Africa to help set up machines at mission hospitals. You can imagine how much this is appreciated. As medical equipment becomes more sophisticated, few on the field are confident in this area. One of her stops was at the ELWA Hospital where a good used machine has been given to replace our original X-ray machine. More short-term help came to put up the extension on the hospital for a larger X-ray department—four young builders— Swanson, Munson, Nelson, and Olson, all from Minnesota!

Picture how many buildings stand across the world in mis sions today because of short-term builders! Churches send crews of lay people to put up churches, dormitories, gyms, or houses. Laymen's groups, such as Men for Missions with OMS International or Wycliffe Associates, work as volunteers for special projects.

We could tell you story after story about short-termers. Often the miracle has been the timing of their arrival. In 1974, we were involved in arrangements for a Medical Group Mission to Liberia sponsored by the Christian Medical Society. There were 160 participants—doctors, dentists, wives, other medical personnel, and general helpers—who descended on us by charter. They spread out across Liberia to work in hospitals, dispensaries, and clinics for the next three weeks. This was no easy task, but it turned out to be a tremendous experience, and was much appreciated by the government and people of Liberia.

Five doctors were assigned to work at the ELWA Hospital, among them a medical student. With this student came her husband. We had not known that he was a plumber. As it turned out, he had one of the most appreciated skills for use right at that time. ELWA had just secured 6,000 feet of plastic piping to replace rusted metal pipes underground around the station.

Just prior to the plumber's arrival, a foreign building contractor had offered ELWA the use of a ditchdigger. When the plumber arrived, he worked for three weeks with the building crew from sunrise to sunset to lay the plastic pipe. When he got on the plane, the job was complete! The next day, the contractor somewhat apologetically came and asked for the ditchdigger, as they had acquired another job! No skills go to waste!

A special group of short-termers are the summer students. With their idealism and enthusiasm, they are a breath of fresh air. There is adjustment on the part of mission personnel to take time to train and encourage young people, but it may be the experience that will encourage the students to consider missions as a real option. Let's not close that door!

Others come in what we might call internships, as they are using the experience to fulfill educational requirements to get more experience. Students from an impressive list of medical schools around the world—many of whom are recipients of a scholarship through MAP International, Inc.—spend about ten weeks in mission hospitals.

We love to hear reports from short-termers who have done

a stint on the mission field, because they have a fresh outlook. They have had the opportunity to see just where they might fit in; and for many, it's an encouragement to the next step of applying for full-time service.

During our first furlough in 1967, a doctor and his wife from the Detroit area spent only three weeks at the ELWA Hospital. As we were praying about returning to the States in 1975 because of our children's needs, this same surgeon and his wife, Frank and Barbara Young, were interested in returning. And they did! They had never gotten over that three-week experience!

## Sending Agencies

Mission agencies are organizations which facilitate sending missionaries to other cultures. The missionaries are then accountable to the agencies. We look through the *Mission Handbook: North American Protestant Ministries Overseas* (12th Edition, Samuel Wilson, Editor, MARC) and we see over 600 agencies listed. The listing includes such information as the primary tasks of the agencies and the number of missionaries. We note that some are very small with few missionaries and some are large. Some work in only one country; others are spread around the world. Some specialize in certain ministries.

A denominational mission board is the agency of the particular church denomination. The missionaries are members of that denomination, and usually the churches founded overseas continue in that group. Home churches include in their budgets money to be sent to the board of missions, and then the board designates how the funds will be used. Missionary contact with the home churches will vary, but it is helpful if the churches get to know missionaries, to more personally pray for their work.

Independent missions draw their personnel from a wide range of denominations and independent churches. The churches planted overseas are not connected with any denomination in the homeland. For example, in Nigeria, the Sudan Interior Mission founded the Evangelical Church of West Africa.

Most interdenominational or independent missions require the missionary to secure his personal support before going to the field. There usually is a close relationship between the missionary and those churches and individuals who are supporting him.

In some cases, missionaries receive exactly what is sent in for their support, while others share in a "pool" system so that there is more equality in support. Missions today, whether denominational or interdenominational, are expected to be run with good business procedures.

## Tentmakers
Some who witness overseas choose to go another route. They are called tentmakers. What makes the tentmaker different from the career missionary is that he is self-supporting through secular employment. He is more than just a Christian businessman overseas, because he is motivated to work in another culture so that he might make Jesus Christ known there. That is his commitment, his calling.

This is not a new way to go with the Gospel. Paul was a tentmaker, providing his own support as a missionary. Paul believed that the Christian worker had the right to be supported by others, as he pointed out in 1 Corinthians 9:14, since this frees the worker to give all his time to the ministry. However, for some reason, Paul chose to support himself. Perhaps he felt he could be a better example, living out his testimony in the business world. Perhaps there were problems in the logistics of receiving the support.

J. Christy Wilson, author of *Today's Tentmakers,* who for years was in Afghanistan as a teacher and chaplain to the international community, has helped many Christians to look at this alternative. Tentmakers go through businesses, universities, government jobs, international organizations, Peace Corps, embassy work, and other ways. The Overseas Counseling Service in Pasadena, California, which helps Christians find jobs abroad, lists over 100,000 job openings. Statistics tell us there are 100 Americans working overseas to every one missionary, so there are great tentmaker opportunities. Students can also study abroad to witness, and some Christians even choose to live part of their retirement years abroad.

To the disadvantage of the tentmaker, his stay in an area usually is not as long as that of a career missionary, so identification with the country and the people is more difficult. He may feel isolated from the culture, if he lives in a community set up by his company. He may not have the fellowship of a band of believers. He may feel frustration of no follow-up of converts when he leaves, no continuity if he is transferred out of the area. He may find it almost impossible in some areas to give a verbal witness. The tentmaker may not have a church in the homeland to which he feels accountable, and which shares with him in praying for his ministry.

On the other hand, the tentmaker is fortunate if a church at home is as supportive in interest and prayers as it is with missionaries who have their financial support. Churches need to realize this also is a way to reach the world.

The self-supporting worker often comes in contact with the elite, the educated, those who know English. As these are introduced to Christ, they can be influential with many others. The tentmaker also can be of special encouragement to the local believers, just as Paul must have been. The tentmaker works side by side with them, facing the same issues and problems, and dealing with them in the context of Christian values. It really helps if he can identify with a local church within the culture.

One great advantage is that a tentmaker can get into countries closed to missions. If the job of reaching the many unreached is to be done, certainly it will take the ingenuity of the tentmaker too.

Missions are encouraging tentmaking and are helping to locate unique places of service. Some missions are training these lay people in Bible study, in cultural insights and methods of reaching out.

Dave and Ruth Van Reken came to Liberia in 1970 for five

months when he was a medical student. Their first child was born there. They tasted the excitement of serving the Lord through a medical work, and after Dave's pediatric residency and a stint in the navy, they returned as medical missionaries. Then came a step to reach out from the ELWA Hospital, as Dave also taught at the University of Liberia Medical School and worked in the John F. Kennedy Medical Center in pediatrics. By his second term, he saw such opportunity to be in on the training of young Liberians that he made the move to go full-time with the Liberian government as professor of pediatrics. What an opportunity he has there in such an important outreach as child health care, and at the same time to be a Christian witness right on the job. He and Ruth also disciple medical students through Bible studies in their home. They still have their relationship with SIM as missionaries, but operate much like tentmakers in the secular work opportunity which is so appreciated by the Liberian government.

A Methodist missionary doctor, Dr. Bill Wallace, worked in the Ministry of Health. We would anticipate that mission agencies might pursue this type of work arrangement where people can be of assistance to a country and where their witness for Jesus Christ can be vital.

The task of world evangelism is so challenging today that it will take the mobilization of all—not just one mission, not just one denomination, not just the traditional career missionary. It is exciting to realize the possibilities for so many to get involved in such a variety of ways!

## Traps Along the Way

With so many choices, where are all the workers? There are many volunteers, but along the road from here to there, some stop. Following God's direction step by step means that God definitely leads some to stay at home. But others are caught in traps along the way and kept from moving on out.

One trap is fear. There is fear of the unknown over against the security of the familiar. There is fear of failure, and this is especially influenced by our success-oriented society. Personal loss of independence when going with a mission organization can be dreaded. Having to raise support can be a frightening prospect, with deputation and speaking assignments lurking in the shadows. The single worker considers the possibility of a lonely life. Married couples wonder if their children will have to be sent away for schooling.

There are other obstacles in the course from here to there. The further one goes in education, the more vocational choices he has. Very attractive offers come along that urge him to stay in his own country. The potential candidate sees the economic gap between his earnings here and his salary as a missionary. That gap continues to widen.

Another obstacle is marriage to a partner who has different goals. Not many Christian parents pray that their children will be called to the mission field. Even committed Christians have difficulty in seeing their children and grandchildren go so far away. It's a subtle obstacle, but a feeling passed on, "Missions are fine—but the missionaries should come from another family."

Dave and Ruth Van Reken prepared a list of principles for medical students planning to go with missions. Their list is valuable for potential missionaries as well. They underscore the problem of debt. Easy credit is a threat. They said, "Realize that you are not living by the same drumbeat as the others in your class. Be very careful about making long-term financial commitments. Keep your debts to an absolute minimum. Realize that you can pay off debts by maintaining a simple lifestyle. Because 'where your treasure is, there will your heart be also,' be cautious about amassing things." Good advice, Dave and Ruth!

The lack of a sense of urgency may slow the pace to the field. Do our churches teach an urgency in getting the message to the world? The atmosphere of No Urgency in relaying the message is a subtle Go Slow sign in getting from here to there.

## Troubles That Bring Them Home

Once on the field, we see that the laborers are too few. Of course, the number of workers is reduced for normal reasons such as retirement, end of a short-term assignment, death, or after service of at least 20 years. But there are other reasons why missionaries who might otherwise have had more productive years leave the work early. What are some of these?

• As a doctor, it was Bob's job to care for missionaries who were having health problems. While the medical picture has greatly improved, poor health is still a major reason people come home. Doctors have to watch for the diseases endemic to a particular area. And missionaries are not immune to cancer and heart disease.

• There are conditions that cause stress. Reaction to stress shows up in physical and mental health, interpersonal relationships, and in the work. We recently read a very interesting study by Myron Loss of Columbia Graduate School of Bible and Missions entitled, "The Missionary's First Term: Crisis in Self-Esteem." His conclusion was that good self-esteem is especially important since the first-term missionary faces an unusual amount of stress. The inability to properly deal with stress is related to early exodus from the field. (This information is now in book form: *Culture Shock,* Light and Life Press.)

Myron Loss measured the missionary's first term by a scale prepared by psychiatrists to determine degrees of stress. The average first-term missionary could easily score way over the danger point. What are some of these threatening changes that produce so much stress? There's the change in financial state, in job, in living conditions, in daily activities and habits, and in language. The first-term missionary might even get married— another stress! There may be a new family member during the first term. There may be illness. These can add up to a dangerously high number of life-change units!

The American first-term missionary has probably never felt so American in his whole life! We recall those stirring moments when we felt our national identity as we walked out on the pier in Monrovia's harbor about two years into our first four-year term. Marian's eyes filled with tears. There were ships from the U.S. Navy with Project Handclasp, and we went on board to meet the captain and some of the crew. They had brought a big shipment of hospital equipment from World Medical Relief of Detroit. The sailors even delivered all the big boxes right out to the station and helped to paint the walls of the building going up. They did this free of any charge, under Project Handclasp. We were so proud to be Americans! There is that crisis of national identity in the first term.

Added to the high number of life-change units that produce stress is the fact that the missionary knows the expectations of those who are standing behind him at home.

Missionaries hate to admit even to one another that they are under stress. Bob recalls one missionary who suffered from stomach ulcers. Bob tried to find out if anything was especially bothering him in his first term. "Not a thing, Doc," was the reply, "the Lord is so gracious." His denial only worsened the problem.

The first-termer needs to know that it takes time to adjust. It has been our observation that missions are working harder at this, preparing candidates for more realistic goals in the first term, and helping them to anticipate the stress they will face.

• Lack of job satisfaction can be another factor. In some places it rests with the missionary to set his own goals, and that's not so easy. Resistance to the Gospel message can be discouraging. A person can also find himself either under-qualified for the job or underchallenged as he moves from place to place in the work. He struggles with the "I'll go any-where and do anything" missionary image. It may be easier for those in measurable work like the medical profession to know just what is to be expected of them, than it is for missionaries in church-planting work.

Some who leave early say they feel pushed out by rigid patterns in missions. They feel they do not have the freedom to be creative and to bring in new ideas.

• Finances can be a burden, especially for large families. Those discouraged by poor support quotas, and who find it difficult to do deputation, may elect to stay home.

• Children's needs bring many home. More and more missionaries are staying home for some important years with children, and possibly returning later to the field. We are among those who have come home for this reason.

• But problems in interpersonal relationships probably cause the most discouragement. Can you imagine what it would be like to do everything with the people you work with? You live close together, you go to church together, you socialize together, you shop together—you just can't get away from the people you work with.

We'll never forget an illustration that Luis Palau gave. He had heard a missionary from rural Mexico say, "Missionaries are like manure. You spread them out around the world and they do a lot of good. But piled up together—they stink!"

Rather than dealing with the interpersonal problems, sometimes missionaries just cover up the difficulties until it is easier to leave than try to solve them.

We are not being critical of those who do return home, for certainly the Lord redirects many in His service. But as encouragers here at home, it is important that we understand some of the particular problems missionaries face and then pray for them, that their years abroad might really be effective, and that their coming back will be at His timing.

## The Challenge to Pray

It is often difficult to know how to pray for missionaries. They can't even write home about some of the situations where they most need your prayers. We are going to suggest five subjects for prayer where you can't go wrong.

• The first is *health*. Many missionaries labor where there are health risks. Pray for their health.

• The second is *compatibility*. There can be so many problems: missionary with missionary, missionary with national, national with national. In Liberia, *palaver* means a problem, disagreement, or anything that has to be talked out. Every village has a palaver hut. The decision finally made is not as important as the opportunity to talk over the problem! We spent many hours listening to missionary palavers over the years. Pray for the missionaries' compatibility.

• The third is *enthusiasm.* We saw missionaries who felt called of God to do a job in Liberia. Some would stick to the goal just like a race horse with blinders. Others would begin to complain: "The food isn't good." "The mission doesn't appreciate what I'm trying to do." "The nationals don't realize what I sacrificed to come." Pretty soon a spirit of pessimism set in like a cancer until it ate away, and the missionary's effectiveness was nil. Pray for their enthusiasm.

• The fourth is the *missionaries' children.* Mother and Father were called of God to serve overseas and the children went along. They have to be careful not to offend anyone, not to hurt the parents' ministry. They have to fit in. Their parents hope they may grow to sense that they are part of the ministry as a family.

Talk to MKs (missionary kids) and you will find most of them love their overseas life. We saw many benefits for our own children. Through contacts with people from such varied backgrounds, we saw them grow to be very accepting of people. They knew what their parents were doing in the work, and even though their father was extremely busy, they felt a part of it. We lived by the ocean, a wonderful spot for boys to play. They had lots of playmates. They went to school right on our station.

But many missionaries have to make other arrangements for schooling for the children. Some take schooling by correspondence; some attend the local public schools or international schools. Some go away from their parents to boarding schools. It is not a simple decision for parents and children, and it certainly must be supported by prayer. Long separations of children from parents can never be easy. Each child is unique. Living away from home affects different children in different ways. For some, it seems to be a good experience, while others find it extremely difficult to cope with the homesickness and loneliness. Years later some children still resent having had to be away from their parents during those early years.

Then there are other adjustments when they return to their

own country. Bob, Jr. and John loved their early years in Liberia, but when they came back to the States on furlough, they would refuse to take anything African for "Show and Tell." They tried hard to be Americans. We observed the struggle. Missionary children look like Americans, but they don't think and act like Americans. Neither are they citizens of the country where they live overseas. They really are in a third culture of their own! Exposed to international opportunities, they have many benefits, but they also have to find their own identity. We are encouraged by efforts made by some missions to give special counsel for children returning to their homeland. Pray for the missionaries' children.

• Lastly, pray for the missionary's *spiritual growth*. The battle is spiritual. Private devotional life is difficult to maintain. Missionaries must be fed spiritually.

If you remember these five things as you pray for the missionaries you know, you can't go wrong: their health, their compatibility, their enthusiasm, their children, and their spiritual growth.

When John was four years old, he used to love to imitate his father who sang bass in the quartet at the station. He'd pull out the piano bench, and standing behind it, he'd throw his head back and sing in his best four-year-old bass. One day Marian did a double take as she heard his version of John Peterson's song—"Surely Goodness and Mercy Shall Follow Me." John sang so lustily, "Surely goodness and emergency shall follow me all the days of my life."

Really, it wasn't so strange. The word was in his small vocabulary as his father was so often called to the hospital for an emergency. And we thought further—in the life of a missionary on the mission field, that's really true too. "Surely goodness and emergency shall follow me." The days are filled with God's goodness and lots of emergencies. That's why we challenge you to pray for the missionaries you know. Pray them through those emergencies, those times of stress, those difficult interpersonal relationships, and on to staying there as long as God wants them to in a life of effective service for Him.

# 7

# Mission Methods

Strategy is set. We have the personnel. The timing seems right. What methods should we use?

There are many methods from which to choose in the work of missions. Some are effective as tools in planting the Word, others in cultivating, and still others for the harvesting. Sometimes they are put to work side by side in the field.

## Evangelism

The heart of missions is evangelism, no matter what method is used. The goal is to plant churches and disciple people. So we need to look more closely at evangelism. In some places it hammers away in a steady manner, slowly getting the job done; in other places it moves like a fire, spreading with immediate results. Evangelism is directed at the yet unreached, those who have not accepted Jesus Christ.

We like an illustration of evangelism told by Dr. Samuel Moffett, missionary statesman who worked in China and Korea for many years. His wife was buying a watermelon from a local vendor in a Korean village. The man was so shocked when he heard her speak in his language that he forgot all about the price and just blurted out, "Are you a Christian?"

"Oh, yes," she answered.

He smiled and said, "Oh, I'm so glad! Because if you weren't, I was going to tell you how much you are missing" ("Evangelism: The Leading Partner," *Perspectives on the World Christian Movement,* eds. Ralph D. Winter and Steven C. Hawthorne, William Carey Library, p. 731).

That's evangelism, telling others the Good News of Jesus Christ, the news that has been missing from their lives. But evangelism also looks for a response.

C. Peter Wagner in *Frontiers in Missionary Strategy* clarifies the three classifications of evangelism which are sometimes given, and shows their relationship in missions—Presence, Proclamation, and Persuasion. He says they are like building blocks that form a total structure of three stories. There is no persuasion without verbal proclamation of the Gospel, and presence gives credibility to proclamation (Moody, p. 134).

The Rutens in Upper Volta live in a mud-brick house on the edge of the Sahara Desert. A big waterpot sits outside the front door, and a thatched-roof porch offers relief from the sun. Hospitality is the key to reaching the Muslim Fulanis, nomadic cattle herders who often stop to visit the Rutens. All three rooms of their house are open for inspection. This is presence evangelism, for by living as Christians in a community of Muslims, the Rutens have made friends.

But it doesn't stop with presence evangelism. As the opportunity comes, they witness. On one occasion, several Fulani students home from the university asked the Rutens, "What do you believe?" That was an open door for proclamation evangelism.

It is a step further to persuasion evangelism. The Rutens are looking for the results, for those who will come to believe. A few among the Fulani Muslims have come to know the Lord ("Out Where It All Begins," *SIM Now,* January-February 1983, pp. 6-7).

In many places it is a slow process and hard work to get past presence evangelism. But in other places large numbers are turning to Christ through evangelism.

Another term that is used is saturation evangelism, which is a concerted effort to present the Gospel in spoken or written form to every individual in every home in the area. Saturation evangelism moves out from the church, training every believer to be an evangelizer. As churches, missions, and denominations cooperate in the outreach, they are strengthened by uniting in spirit and in activities toward a common goal.

This kind of evangelism has gone by different titles in various areas of the world, but there is similarity among the movements. The first, Evangelism in Depth, was the idea of Dr. Kenneth Strachan of the Latin America Mission, with the first campaign in Nicaragua in 1960. This moved out across other parts of Latin America. New Life for All, under the leadership of Gerry Swank of SIM, followed in Nigeria in 1963, and then moved into other African countries. In Zaire, it was called Christ for All. Korea followed with the National Evangelistic Campaign, Japan with Mobilization Evangelism, the Philippines with the Christ the Only Way Movement, and Vietnam with Evangelism Deep and Wide. All of these movements reaped a large number of converts for Christ.

Parades and rallies were part of the New Life for All strategy in Nigeria. There was political tension in a Benue town in eastern Nigeria in the 1960s when a parade was scheduled. Pastor Yakuba had a premonition that something spectacular might happen. Would it be a riot or a blessing?

After the parade, Pastor Yakuba stood in the marketplace and gave the message. As he asked the great number gathered how many wanted to accept Jesus Christ as Saviour, he was not prepared for what happened. A sea of hands went up.

Pastor Yakuba explained again, but the response only grew larger! Then he made it even harder. He said, "If you are really sincere, you will follow the Christians to the church and confess your sins to God there."

The crowd swelled as they marched to the church which could hardly contain them.

"Are some of these Christians?" he asked.

"No, they are all pagans," he was told. "They want new life in Christ." And some 500 were shown the way to Christ (Eileen Lageer, *New Life for All*, Moody, pp. 64-65).

New Life for All workers went on to say that it seemed God had been preparing the hearts of many in the district so that *whole tribes were ready to turn to Christ.*

Whole tribes? That's something for individualistic Americans to stop and consider! Let's look at another movement in missions—the Church Growth Movement. Dr. Donald McGavran, former missionary to India and founder of the School of World Missions and Church Growth, has been a spokesman for this concept.

McGavran says evangelism should bring increased numbers of churches as disciples are made. If this isn't happening, there must be a reevaluation of the methods. McGavran says we should look at the churches that are multiplying and learn from them. The emphasis is on planning for church growth.

Church growth principles emphasize that work should be done among people who are receptive. Communication of the Gospel in a way that is understandable to the culture is important. The movement recognizes that it is possible and desirable to see conversions of whole groups of people to Christianity.

Let's examine more closely the concept of a whole group or tribe coming to Christ. This is foreign to our thinking, but in some cultures, most of the important decisions are made by the elders of the tribes or families. This fits into the pattern of life for Asian, African, and South American societies. Christianity may seem to them an invading religion, and so it is all the more important that the group enter into the decision to turn to Christianity. Paul Hiebert, Professor of Anthropology and South Asian Studies at the School of World Missions says, "Group decisions do not mean that all members of the group are converted, but it does mean that the group is open to further biblical instruction. The task of the missionary is not finished; it has only begun, for he must now teach the whole of Scriptures" ("Social Structure and Church Growth," *Perspectives on the World Christian Movement,* eds. R.D. Winter and S.C. Hawthorne, William Carey Library, p. 386).

Twenty-five heads of families in an Islamic village in Africa recently brought a letter to a pastor. It said, "We, the undersigned, and our families, have decided to follow Jesus Christ. We want you to help us." An emphasis on individual decisions tends to force people to live outside of their own culture if their conversion to Christianity cannot be tolerated by their people. Groups of Christians can be supportive of one another and make it possible to live within the culture as a witness.

Group conversions are not new. Joshua said, "As for me and my household, we will serve the Lord" (Josh. 24:15). When the Philippian jailer responded to the Gospel, he and his household were baptized (Acts 16:29-34). Clusters of people, people movements to Christ—that is the vision of church growth in populations where this is the normal pattern for life's decisions. While a few converts come one by one, the harvest is expected to yield whole clusters too.

## Church Planting

As evangelism is the heart of missions, so church planting is the foundation of missions. By this we mean more than the visible structure of the church.

Early in the 1960s we flew in a single-engine mission plane for some 200 miles over the deep jungle growth of the interior of Liberia and visited the Lutheran hospital at ZorZor. It was a learning situation for us, as our hospital was not yet built. Betty, the doctor's wife, wanted to share with us an experience she thought we would appreciate. It was already dark on a Sunday evening when we followed her down the lantern-lit path. We walked through a thick growth of trees and in the stillness of the evening came to a clearing. There we saw a small structure, several poles pounded into the ground and a thatched roof of palm branches. Inside were a few handmade low benches.

This was the structure, but it really wasn't the church. As we waited, one by one the people came, some needing assistance. We couldn't even see them clearly in the dim light. Then the service began, the Loma tunes punctuated by the drumbeat. A few stood to give testimony and we felt our hearts respond. Though we could not understand the Loma language, we heard the "uh-huhs" in agreement, and we felt like joining in. This was the church—this body of believers in a village for leprosy patients.

Missions are asking for more church planters to work with unreached peoples, to establish churches which will multiply themselves out into the culture. Career missionaries are best suited for this challenging work. Friendships must be made, the language learned, the culture appreciated, and the Gospel communicated. As the church planter gives guidance and instruction through God's Word, he moves wisely within the culture so that new believers can see what to retain and what to discard, without taking on the trappings of Western ways.

## Bible Teaching
This brings us to another tool in missions—Bible teaching. What would happen if your church grew from 100 to 500 members in a year? And we don't mean people who have just moved from one church to the other church, like they do here. We mean really new believers, most of them from a pagan background. What would happen if your church multiplied from one to five churches in two years? "Great!" you say. But can you foresee any problems? Where would you find enough trained leaders? Might there be chaos? If enough churches grew this way, it could be a problem, even in the United States where there are many seminaries, Bible schools, and Christian colleges.

Explosive growth has taken place around the world, and like SIM says about some fields in Africa, "The church is in flood. Spiritual disaster looms large unless pastoral training can keep pace with the rate of growth" (SIM Now, July-August 1982, p. 3).

Mission leaders tell us that our failure to produce enough well-trained leaders has been a weakness in missions for years. The new churches face a theological battle. In some places it is not just a battle with liberal theology, but also with the problem of syncretism. We mentioned contextualization before, which is seeking to communicate the truth of the Bible so that it is real in a given culture. While contextualization and syncretism might appear related, they are quite different. Syncretism combines beliefs of other religions or pagan customs with Christianity. This attempt has been made especially where Christianity is viewed as a Western religion which has invaded a culture. There is a tremendous need for clear biblical understanding at this point.

Theological seminaries, Bible schools, and colleges have existed over the years on mission fields, but in few places have they been able to keep up with the need. Missions have offered scholarships for national leaders to attend Western institutions. While many have benefited from the excellent training, there is a hardship in being transported out of their own countries, away from families. Further, it has been noted that there is a tendency to minister mostly in the cities when they return home.

Countries that in the past have been on the receiving end of missions are establishing their own institutions. But still, there is a need for more Bible training. Have you heard of TEE? You don't have to look far in mission literature these days before you'll read something about it.

The Presbyterian Church of Guatemala was the first to put this idea together. They faced a shortage of church leaders and saw those trained in seminaries moving to the cities. In 1960 they took a good look at their methods, their North American curriculum, and their institutions that required the students to leave home to study. Why not take the theological education to the student, where he is living? TEE was born—Theological Education by Extension.

There is a lot to say in favor of TEE. Usually the students are married and they can continue to support their families at home. If they already are pastors, they can stay with their churches. The training is practical; they can immediately use what they learn. In most places, a workbook and textbook give guidance to the Bible study; but where students are illiterate, the studies are programmed through cassettes. TEE is a powerful and practical tool for Bible teaching in missions.

"Government Schools Need Bible Teachers," was a headline that caught our eye. Can you imagine that situation? Unusual opportunities come for teaching Bible in the government schools of some countries! Where there's a keen desire for education, Bible correspondence courses also are popular. Bible teaching is a building tool in missions.

## Translation

When the Scriptures are not in the language of the people, it is necessary to translate them. Wycliffe Bible Translators has been the leader in this. It was a young man by the name of W. Cameron Townsend who stepped out with the new vision of the importance of translation of the Scriptures. As a student volunteer, he went to Guatemala in the early 1930s to help the churches already there. He was struck with the fact that most of the people did not speak Spanish. Cam was challenged with a question from an Indian, "If your God is so smart, why can't He speak our language?"

Townsend was determined, with the Lord's help, to reach the tribal people by putting the Bible in their own language. From this vision came the Wycliffe Bible Translators. The organization now numbers over 4,000 workers, and is still addressing the challenge of translating the Scriptures into some 3,000 languages and dialects.

What would your response to the Gospel be if you couldn't hear it or read it in your own language? In the Paez Church in the central Colombian Andes, few believers ever stayed for the Lord's Supper observance at the end of their annual conference. The Scripture was always read in Spanish, "This is My body which was given for you."

Then one year a Christian and Missionary Alliance missionary asked some Wycliffe translators if there was any Scripture translated into Paez which included the Lord's Supper. A book, *The Life of Christ,* written in Paez did include the Luke 22 account.

That year when Paez was read in the Communion service, hundreds of believers stayed. "Before," a church leader said, "most of us understood very little in Spanish. But now we understand that His body and His blood were given for us, and we happily receive it. Who wouldn't?" ("In Open Words," *Jubilee,* Vol. 7, No. 6, Summer 1981, Wycliffe, p. 11)

Linguists live close to the people. For months they listen carefully for the different sounds, then analyze them and record them. The selection of a helper from the local language group to assist in the work is very important. Translation work is tedious. The right words are chosen. When there is no equivalent word, the translator may choose to use a word that conveys a similar idea. Different cultural patterns can add confusion. It is not easy work and takes many years.

But do you want to hear something really exciting? The modern computer has entered the picture, trimming years off translation work! We were visiting SIM headquarters in New Jersey where we saw translators who worked in the bush areas in Africa coming back to learn how to use word processors and computers! This has been coordinated with information from Wycliffe, the pioneers in the use of the computer in translation work. The word processor can be taken where electricity is not available, to run on diesel or solar power.

We met an older missionary who had been called from a retirement center in California. She was a Hausa language expert and was learning to use the word processor so that she could make corrections on Hausa translations sent to her.

They explained to us how simple it would be to make corrections. If one letter in a word is changed, the correction need only be made once, and it will be corrected throughout the manuscript. This replaces the months of tedious recopying. We were amazed as we watched the alphabetizing, indexing, and other steps so quickly done by computer. The completed translation tapes are sent to printers who feed the tapes right into computerized presses, cutting possibilities of errors so easily made when setting type in an unfamiliar language. You can see where years will be cut out of the translation process!

Literacy classes are often conducted along with the translation of a language, teaching illiterates to read. As a result, the literacy rate in the particular language group rises way above the national average!

Some places don't wait until they can read! In Ethiopia some 2,300 Bible study groups were meeting around tape players to hear Scripture read in the Wolayta language! There were some 30,000 people studying the Bible each week! Now, that's a Bible study! (Africa Now, SIM, November-December 1980)

For minds eager for education, there never seems to be enough reading material. Literature is a powerful tool—books, magazines, tracts. A missionary writes of selling over 400 books in one afternoon!

## Radio

There is another mighty voice and that is radio. The sign-on signal for ELWA each day is from the hymn, "Give the Winds a Mighty Voice." That is truly the influence of radio around the world.

HCJB of Quito, Ecuador, the pioneer in missionary short-wave radio, began in 1931. Far East Broadcasting Company, Trans World Radio, and ELWA followed, and all together these four blanket much of the world. Smaller stations operated by missions target particular areas. Governments have even opened up time, sometimes free of charge, for religious broadcasting on their stations.

At the ELWA Hospital, we had pillow speakers so that patients could select broadcasts in their own Liberian language, or French or English. It was thrilling to look out at the towering antennas and realize that the air waves were carrying the message of Jesus Christ at the same time to the rest of Liberia, on through other parts of Africa, and right on behind the closed doors of northern Africa. That is one of the unique advantages of radio.

On a furlough trip home, we stopped in North Africa where we met a man who prepared broadcasts for ELWA. He would go over into Spain to prepare the programs and send the tapes to ELWA. The broadcasts would then be beamed back to the Muslim world of North Africa. He told us that when he went out on the street he was careful not to talk a lot. He knew he had a listening audience over radio when someone would say, "I recognize your voice; aren't you the man who talks on the radio?"

Alex Leonovich of Slavic Missionary Society and TWR broadcaster to Russia, reported on a recent visit there. He said, "Over and over again people would come to us and say, 'We heard your programs.' " He was told that out of 12,000 recent converts baptized, 80 percent had heard the Gospel first on radio and then had sought churches (TWR, Vol. 3, No. 2, 1982, p. 15).

Far East Broadcasting Company claims they get many letters from China in response to their Golden Age program which is designed especially for the youth. A Seminary of the Air from Hong Kong is broadcast into China for biblical training of leaders of the house churches.

Radio can prepare the way for the missionary too. Opening up a work in a new village, a missionary in Brazil traveled there in his river launch. A crowd gathered and he started to tell them of Jesus Christ. But he was interrupted by one of the villagers who said, "This is not new to us, but you go ahead." He was caught by surprise and asked, "Who told you?" And then he learned that they listened regularly on their little transistor radio to Christian broadcasts (TWR, February 1982, p. 15).

Follow-up is important. Letters are answered by counselors who share literature. Bible correspondence courses may be offered.

A drawback for the modern tool of radio is the high cost for equipment, the price of fuel for power, and the constant maintenance. Specialized people are needed, and so it can be more difficult to nationalize ministries.

New technology will enhance the power of radio, and television is entering the picture in many places along with radio. But not every place has TV on mission fields, and films are very effective. In Ghana, for example, two Cinema Vans go out into the towns. Crowds gather wherever the equipment is set up, sometimes on football fields. Each van moves on to about 20 different places in a month. In a recent month, over 220,000 attended the film showings.

Radio, TV, films, cassettes, and even recordings played on hand-crank machines are part of the mass-media presentation of the Gospel to the world.

Youth camps offer another way to share the Gospel overseas, and Word of Life Fellowship has moved out from its camping headquarters in New York to camping programs in Kenya, Germany, Portugal, Brazil, Argentina, Mexico, Australia, and the Philippines! Each camp is a miracle story and confronts the energy of youth with the energy of the Gospel.

We don't lack for tools in missions. The task is to use the right ones at the right times in the right places—some for planting, some for cultivating, some for harvesting, to gather the fruit "from every nation, tribe, people, and language" (Rev. 7:9).

# 8

# Ministries of Concern

"He went around doing good" (Acts 10:38).

Peter was at the home of Cornelius and was speaking of Jesus Christ. Cornelius' relatives and friends had gathered to listen to everything that Peter could tell them in his first house meeting with Gentiles.

Peter told them how Jesus had conducted His ministry. As He passed by the sick, the lame, and the blind, He showed concern. He touched them and healed them. He released those oppressed by Satan. He was concerned for the hungry and He fed them. He taught, often in parables, that the people might understand. He taught lessons on human value. His ultimate act of concern was laying down His life for others.

Jesus' lifestyle was consistent with His message of reconciliation. And when Jesus gave His followers instructions for their first Gospel team effort, He told them to also go about doing good. He added, "Freely you have received, freely give" (Matt. 10:8).

As followers of Jesus Christ, we too find ourselves involved in works of concern. In some places in this suffering world, physical or social needs may be so great that there can be no compassion in speaking of God's love without first showing concern for temporal needs. Social concern is not bait for the message to follow. The more we learn of Christ, the more we see His genuine concern for the whole person—mind, emotion, body, and spirit. Our concern should be consistent with the message that we share, God's redeeming love through Jesus Christ. Like the disciples, freely we have received, and so freely we share through these ministries of concern.

## Education

General education was taken by early missionaries wherever they went. Starting a school could mean entrance into a country. Mission schools were established at all levels, elementary through university, along with some trade schools. During the days of colonization in Africa, much of the education was left to missions. Their schools were recognized for high academic standards, good discipline, and character training. Many prominent leaders were educated in mission schools. Students sought the Western curriculum as a step toward the outside world.

Through the years, trained nationals have replaced missionaries as teachers in these schools. As countries have nationalized, governments have taken over the educational responsibilities, and national churches now operate many of the mission schools. Today, missions place less emphasis on institutions for general education. Instead, the trend has been to cooperate with nationalization, and in some cases, to supply missionary teachers when requested.

There still are some schools for missionary children, a number of them cooperative efforts of several missions. Many of these schools take students outside of the mission family, so that an international community exists right in the classroom.

Teaching English as a second language is a specialized educational tool. These classes hold potential in closed-door countries, because English is still a language desired around the world. This tool is especially useful in the hands of a short-term missionary or tentmaker.

## Medicine

Medical assistance is another tool that the early missionaries took with them. Probably nothing speaks more clearly of concern than alleviating suffering and caring for physical needs. It is a long way from the few and meager remedies that went with the pioneer missionaries, to sophisticated medical institutions built by missions. In recent years, however, there has been a change of emphasis in medical missions.

A few nurses started a clinic at ELWA in Liberia soon after the opening of the radio work, because they saw overwhelming needs. Government facilities were not adequate. But the clinic did not remain small, and so they prayed and planned for a doctor and a hospital.

We arrived at ELWA, and Bob began to work along with the nurses at the clinic. As our barrels arrived, Bob improvised with tubing he had brought along to try to save babies who were dehydrated and near death. He made house calls to the villages in the middle of the night. Just out of residency, he felt the pressure of caring for missionaries with facilities that seemed so primitive. There were increased demands as local people learned there was a doctor at ELWA.

The hospital was completed in three years, and the work increased even more! But we cannot go farther without sharing some of this miracle story of the building of the hospital. You recall that the general manager at ELWA had assured us, "This life of faith is terrific," when he told us that there were no funds, no equipment, and only a few nurses for a hospital to be built as we were preparing to leave for Liberia.

Bob had finished his surgery residency in July 1962, and we had asked people to pray that we might be in Africa by October. Word came to us that Back to the Bible broadcast of Lincoln, Nebraska—which ELWA aired five times a day throughout Africa—was presenting one wing of the ELWA Hospital for $10,000 as a project for their missionary broadcasts in August. They mentioned this project only five minutes on their broadcast every Monday in August. We visited their studios, and Bob spoke about the vision of the hospital. But our faith was small.

We didn't think it was possible to get $10,000 as a result of just four programs—and only five minutes in each.

In September the letter came from Back to the Bible, "It doesn't look as though we will be sending $10,000." We thought, "Uh-huh, that's what we expected!" But we read on, "Instead we will be sending over $30,000!" In 1962, that was a lot of money!

The letter went on to tell how the first $10,000 had come from many listeners giving smaller gifts. The second wing was a gift of $10,000 from a farmer and his wife in Nebraska. They had sold their farm as they were retiring, and with the consent of their family, they gave a tithe.

But the third donation was even more unusual. It was from an 86-year-old black Christian lady from Edna, Texas. Mrs. Josephine Carmichael told Back to the Bible that her grandfather had come from Liberia as a slave, from a line of native doctors. Her sister had been a missionary to Liberia but had to return home because of health reasons. Mrs. Carmichael wanted "to help her people in Liberia." A few weeks later she sent an additional $5,000 to the SIM headquarters to help equip her wing.

Mrs. Carmichael was a retired schoolteacher. She said that her husband had made some money buying land, but that he hadn't spent his money wisely. When he died, she decided to give the money to the Lord.

When the story behind this gift was told at the ELWA Hospital dedication in 1965, the late President of Liberia, William V. S. Tubman, spontaneously and publicly extended an invitation, "I want Mrs. Carmichael to visit Liberia, and she can live as a guest at the Executive Mansion for the rest of her life if she chooses!"

She wanted to come, but the health of the companion who was to travel with her would not allow it. So the Liberian Ambassador to the United States flew from Washington to Texas. As the bands played and the town gathered for the event, Ambassador Peale conferred on Mrs. Carmichael one of Liberia's highest decorations, Knight Grand Commander of the Humane Order of African Redemption.

On our first furlough, it was Bob's privilege to go to the little town of Edna. There he met Mrs. Josephine Carmichael, a small, stooped, and very gracious Christian woman, then 91 years of age. Her surroundings offered no indication of her ability to give $15,000 toward the building of a hospital. She had literally given her all to help her people in Africa.

Bob plugged the slide projector into the ceiling socket in a small hallway, and showed her the miracle story of the ELWA Hospital. A contented smile stayed on her face. She could have chosen to keep the money and watch it grow, or to spend it on her home, but she chose what she felt was a better way.

Bob went away very humbled. He felt he had been in the presence of a giant of faith. She had given so much for the ELWA Hospital. As he flew back to Michigan in the evening sunset, he dedicated his life anew to the task the Lord had given him to do in Liberia.

Medical institutions were built in missions around the world. Some of them specialized in particular areas, such as eye work or leprosy care. The help has usually been greatly appreciated by the host countries.

Training has been a key to effectiveness. Mission hospitals train nurses, lab technologists, nurses' aides, and even doctors. Medical work offers the opportunity of discipling Christian staff members. It also offers a unique opportunity for verbal witness to patients along with the caring witness. The patient is not just a captive audience, but may really be listening. In Liberia, we called it Medicine with a Message.

Running a medical institution in a developing country is a tremendous challenge. At the ELWA Hospital, we knew it was impossible to have everything, and yet we continued to trust God to supply our needs. Most mission hospitals could not exist without help from organizations such as MAP, which collect and send out donated drugs and supplies at the cost of handling.

For us, it was a continued exercise of faith that we would have the right drugs and supplies at the right time. We recall how much we counted on our X-ray machine, something we take for granted here. We even had the opportunity to get an extra one when a friend of ours, a doctor with the U.S. Embassy, asked if we could use a portable X-ray machine. He was getting rid of his office equipment in New Hampshire where he had been in private practice. He wanted to give the portable to us.

We really looked forward to receiving the machine. But then as the months dragged out, we knew it must be lost at sea.

Then one day our big X-ray machine stopped working, something we had always dreaded. We found it was a major problem which would take several months to fix, since parts were needed from Germany. But that very afternoon, the ELWA truck pulled up to the hospital with a huge crate from port! You guessed it—it was the portable X-ray machine! We plugged it in, and it worked! We didn't lose a day for X rays. We were always so conscious of God's provision at the ELWA Hospital.

Through the years we saw the medical work grow. The more the staff cared for the people, the more sick were brought. The better the reputation of good medicine, the more came. And so the work increased and the staff was overworked. They were often frustrated by the lack of time to be involved in more direct spiritual ministries.

We also saw changes in the country. When we first went to Liberia, we could count on the fingers of one hand the number of national doctors there. But through the years, we saw increased and better government facilities. More Liberian doctors came back after training abroad, and a local medical school was beginning to produce its own doctors.

This has been the story of medical missions around the world, with changes in roles and emphasis. Missions have been looking carefully at their medical work and asking questions. The shortage of personnel seems to be a constant problem. There is the frustration of "spinning the wheels," working night and day, and never even scratching the surface of what needs to be done. It is difficult to turn anyone away. Patients come from great distances, and there is little opportunity to build lasting relationships. What happens when the patient returns to his village far away? The financial burden of the medical work can be a drain on other endeavors on the field. With rising costs of medicine and equipment around the world, missions are asking questions: Is the hospital too big a burden for the national church or the host government ever to run? Is the technology too sophisticated for the setting?

Missions also ask: What are the goals of medical missions? Is the work accomplishing its original purpose, that of evangelism, discipleship, and church planting? Should preventative medicine and community health replace the institutions, or should they work together?

There still is tremendous need for the compassion of healing ministries. "Health for All by the Year 2000" was the slogan adopted by representatives of 134 nations who met in 1978 for the World Health Organization and UNICEF. We have seen figures that say that 80 to 90 percent of the world's population is still without access to basic health care.

The gap seems to be widening between those who have good health care and those in the developing world who have so little. But there is a new direction given to medical missions these days. While there still is a need for curative centers at the hospitals, missions also are focusing on the prevention of disease and the promotion of good health care at the community level by going out to the people where they live.

In a community health team, the responsibility is shared with others and does not fall just on the professional. While the doctors or nurses oversee the programs, they do not have to be involved every day.

In some places, the health workers are elected from the community, people who are already accepted by the village. They are trained in basic health services, and taught to treat the most common diseases. They instruct the villagers in how to get rid of sources of contamination. They teach good nutrition. Periodic visits to the medical center upgrade the village worker's health education. Pastors and other Christian workers can carry on a spiritual ministry as members of the team.

Storytelling has been a very effective means of teaching

good health care, especially in Africa where this is already a common method of teaching. Dr. David Hilton, who left hospital work in Nigeria to work in community health, has developed a program using stories.

Community health care—this is the new direction given to medical missions. Going right into the villages where the health problems exist makes sense. Usually this is done under a government program. Does this mean that there is no longer need for hospital work? No, while there are few mission hospitals being built anymore, there still is need for a medical center from which the community health programs can work.

## Community Development

Did you know that chickens, fish ponds, palm trees, and tea all have something in common in missions? They are products of the tool of *agriculture,* a significant piece of mission equipment. With 75 to 80 percent of third world people dependent on the soil for livelihood, and with droughts, famines, and increased population pointing to a world shortage of food, attention has been drawn to improving agriculture.

This is not a new tool. Wherever missionaries have gone, they have carried seeds, planted trees, and introduced methods. But in recent years, efforts have been strengthened to help people produce enough to take care of themselves. Terms like crop rotation, animal husbandry, grain storage, and irrigation are part of mission language. Agriculturists and veterinarians are part of the team. These specialists learn to listen to the local people, to build on what has been done in the past, to make use of their suggestions. They act as liaisons between the government and research centers and the local people.

Industrial trades are also mission tools. Welding, typing, sewing, carpentry, leatherwork, weaving, and printing are only some of the things taught. The goal is that the quality of life be improved and that people become self-reliant.

Some missions have found that the best way to do this is to combine these effective tools—education, health care, agriculture, trades—and then put them in the hands of the people and call it Community Development. There's a special twist in this—the community itself is really involved in using the tools. Let's look at this concept.

Developers do not come with all the answers to problems. The local people are to be involved in identifying and solving the problems. Those who work on community development teams include people with administrative and technical skills and gifts in evangelism and church planting. Some of the needs considered are water, sanitation, food supply, income, clothing, health, and education.

Take, for instance, the matter of water. In some places the problem is the shortage, and in other places, it's pollution. Gordon Comstock, Director of Administration of MAP, tells of a visit to Ecuador. High on a mountain ridge south of Quito, he stood with a Christian Quichua Indian who pointed to a school in the valley below and told Gordon this story. Several years ago, 16 children who attended the school suddenly became violently ill with high fever, abdominal pain, and diarrhea. It was typhoid fever, and they died. No one thought to relate it to the school's source of drinking water, the stream nearby where at recess the children would run to get a cool drink. That same stream drained the barnyards upstream. It was also a clothes washer and a bathtub. From time to time, there were similar deaths.

Through the years, many of the villagers became Christians, and through the work of the Gospel Missionary Union, they gradually became interested in improving their living conditions. Their attention was drawn to the stream as the source of disease. Then MAP was asked to assist in helping the village leaders to plan and build a good water system (*MAP International Report,* February-March 1983).

MAP only helped, for the project had to belong to the community. This is a must in the philosophy of community development. The community gets involved in life-changing improvements. It may take the form of digging wells, of building storage tanks for rain water. It may mean increased income from raising chickens and selling eggs, from improved farming, from basketry or pottery. It may mean learning carpentry or beekeeping. It may mean building storage granaries. Immunizations are given, and good health habits are taught by the village health worker. Literacy classes may be going on at the same time. This is community development.

It might look like a small scratch on the surface of the world's problems. But every bit helps and host countries are very appreciative. Ideally, this works best within a community of Christian believers who will show they are caring. But when a church is not present, it may open up church-planting opportunities. There's a trust built into this relationship. Because life becomes more meaningful, the Gospel is more understandable.

## Relief Work

There's still another specialized tool of concern, and that's relief work. Disasters strike—earthquakes, droughts, floods. Famines leave thousands destitute and starving. Wars and political upheavals leave others wandering and homeless. Crisis after crisis calls for emergency relief. While governments do step in, missions also provide aid where they are working. There are Christian relief agencies which specialize in this ministry, offering relief and then rehabilitation.

One of these is the World Relief Camp Mocoron in Honduras. Thousands of Miskito Indians had fled northeastern Nicaragua. Their homes and fields, and even the Moravian churches where many of them had worshiped, had been burned to the ground in the political tension of that region. They fled across the river into the flatlands of Honduras. The Honduras government requested World Relief's help. Every day the Indians streamed into the camp at Mocoron.

World Relief contacted medical suppliers, called for more workers, organized a shipment of tents, and brought in 30 tons of food per week. Vaccinations were given to curb disease. Pipes were laid to a clean water supply, and three milk feeding stations for children, two clinics, and a nutrition center were organized in the camp. Roads had to be built to connect the camp to an airstrip and port. Another goal was yet to be faced:

resettling the Indians in eastern Honduras.

A relief worker watched the Indians gather to worship in the camp; "They stood, some barefoot, under a canvas roof, their voices accompanied only by the wind. . . . They found cause for praise. They were alive. They had food and clothes. God was faithful" (*Touching,* World Relief, Summer 1982, p. 12).

This same cross-cultural concern continues here as churches and individuals help to sponsor and relocate refugees who immigrate to America.

## Aviation

There are tools that stand by to give assistance when needed, and aviation is one of these. Think of the stories that planes could tell! There's the missionary child's flight to boarding school. There are flights to important conferences and deliveries of supplies and mail. There are emergency medical flights. Ernie Doerksen grew up as an MK in Zaire when it was the Belgian Congo and later returned with Missionary Aviation Fellowship.

Ernie knew the importance of good flying skills and well-maintained aircraft, but he also knew the power of prayer to guide the pilot. He tells of one particular time.

"I had been on a flight to a mission station about 400 miles from home base. On the way back, I flew over a town where missionaries Philip and Edith Cochran of the Assemblies of God were stationed."

Ernie didn't know that the Cochran's radio transmitter receiver had been out of order for days. That was the only way they had contact with the outside world.

Ernie continued, "I was about to fly over their station when I felt a strong compulsion to turn around and land at the airstrip. As I taxied up, I saw Philip's pickup come bouncing down the road. But when the pickup came to a halt, it was Mrs. Cochran who got out and ran to the plane."

"Ernie," she said, "you're the answer to our prayers." Her husband had been seriously ill for days, but she had no way to summon help. But Mrs. Cochran explained, "Somehow I knew that you'd be flying in this area today, and I spent the whole morning on my knees, praying to the Lord that you'd stop."

Philip Cochran was close to death when he got to the hospital, but his eventual recovery testifies to the combination of prayer and medicine and God's place for pilots and planes in missions (Lee Roddy, *On Wings of Love,* Thomas Nelson Publishers, pp. 95-96).

## The Bottom Line
There are other tools that are not so visible, but without which missions could not do the job. In the background are the unsung heroes who are in administration and the business offices, the bookkeepers, the computer operators, the secretaries. There are the guesthouse hosts and hostesses. There are builders, maintenance and service people. There are hostel parents at schools.

The list of those in supportive ministries is long. These are the people who help tighten the bolts and hold it all together, to insure that the message really gets out.

THE EPICUREAN

SO I SAID, LOOK, DO YOU HAVE TO DRAG RELIGION INTO EVERY-THING? CAN'T YOU JUST FEED PEOPLE WITHOUT PREACHING TO THEM? CAN'T YOU JUST GIVE THEM FOOD AND MEDI-CINE AND CLOTHING AND THEN GO HELP SOMEBODY ELSE?

AND HE SAID, YOU MEAN BREAD ALONE?

SIM

**Figure 5**

For that's the bottom line—does the message get out? Sometimes in the desire to put all of our good programs to work, in the heat of the battle and the fatigue of overwork, we have to stop again and ask—Is the message getting through?

We told you before of the Medical Group Mission that came to Liberia for three weeks in 1974 with over 160 participants. We were quite proud of how things were going, as the medical personnel spread throughout the country. No real problems, and Liberia was most appreciative of the tremendous help.

Five of the doctors were assigned to ELWA. One doctor examined a man who complained of a headache and prescribed malaria treatment. But the man just sat there. Next, the visiting doctor gave him some aspirin. And the man continued to sit there.

Finally, thinking that he must have missed something, the doctor asked the man, "Is there anything else?"

The man looked at him and asked, "Aren't you Christian Medical Society?"

"Oh, yes," the doctor replied, and with pride he pointed to his name tag with Christian Medical Society printed on it.

"Aren't you going to tell me about Jesus Christ?" the man asked him.

That struck us all like a ton of bricks—"Aren't you going to tell me about Jesus Christ?"

With our tools of concern, we still need to get back to our priorities and be sure that the message comes through loud and clear. Medicine—education—agriculture—community development—relief work—tools of concern—all with a message!

"Aren't you going to tell me about Jesus Christ?"

# 9

# Missions from the Non-Western World

We are not alone. A new enforcement is already at the front lines. We do not face the challenge of evangelization of the world by ourselves. This is good news!

There are already over 15,000 in this rapidly growing force. They are continuing to march out to the front from all over the world. Where are they coming from? These are missionaries from the areas of the world labeled third world or non-Western. This designation is for nations not aligned with either of the two great powers, and usually refers to countries in Africa, Asia, and Latin America.

As a body, these new enforcements are called third world missions. They are coming from third world churches. The receiving churches have become sending churches. Missiologist C. Peter Wagner states that missions have come full circle—360 degrees! At 90 degrees, the mission sent out missionaries to a certain people. At 180 degrees, people came to Christ and a church was planted, but the church was under the mission's supervision. At 270 degrees, the church became autonomous and took care of its own affairs. Now, at 360 degrees, the receiving church becomes a sending church through a mission of its own (*On the Crest of the Wave*, Regal, pp. 164-165).

These missions are recruiting workers five times faster than their Western counterparts. They are experiencing phenomenal growth! Their missionaries are coming from churches that are experiencing explosive expansion and that well may pass the Western churches in numbers by the year 2000.

It's only been in the last ten years that we have heard much about this mission force. When we began to teach mission classes in 1975, we referred to earlier figures which showed there were some 3,000 missionaries in third world missions. Today we refer to figures from the early 1980s which speak of over 15,000, one-third of the present Western Protestant force, and that figure is increasing.

Why didn't this happen sooner? Have we as Western missions been partly responsible? Have we been careful enough to pass on the command of the Great Commission to the new churches? Have they sensed their responsibility to reach out? Have we encouraged them to stay in their Jerusalem because there was so much to be done there? Have we offered the receiving churches the option of sending?

Because the nature of the Christian church is mission, there have been earlier mission efforts from the third world too. For instance, Burmese missionary societies were formed 150 years ago. Joseph Merrick went from Jamaica to Cameroon in Africa in 1843. In the early nineteenth century, a cross-cultural missionary in the Pacific took the Gospel to the islands of Oceania, and in 1835, when the first European missionary went there, he found 2,000 native Christians meeting in 65 villages! Since then, over 1,000 Pacific Islanders have gone out as missionaries. The church *is* mission!

Over in Guadalcanal another mission, the Melanesian Brotherhood, began in 1925. God called out a young man named Ini Kopuria from one of the small villages there. He had been trained in missionary schools and served in the army. Recovering from an accident while in the service, he heard God say to him, "All this I gave to you; what have you given to Me?"

Ini dedicated his life to the ministry. His dream was to take the Gospel to every village where he had gone, during his army days, to seek out prisoners. In 1925 he sought the counsel of an Anglican Bishop to organize the Melanesian Brotherhood.

Others joined Ini to reach their fellow islanders and those beyond. They divided into small groups and walked barefoot throughout the islands. Their numbers grew, and they reached out to other islands and even Papua, New Guinea. Over 100 missionaries were sent out in the 15 years prior to the Second World War. Although Ini had died, the Brotherhood picked up their mission after the war, and some 9,500 became Christians from 1955 to 1975.

The national believers supported this mission. From the churches, a group known as a Company of Companions stood behind them in prayer. The youth organized the Copra Brothers to support the work by gathering coconuts and making copra, dried coconut meat. Lawrence Keyes says, "In short, the Melanesian Brotherhood became the heroes of the national church" (Keyes, *The Last Age of Missions,* William Carey Library, pp. 94-97).

## Today's Enforcements

From what countries do we see them coming today? Some of the latest information has been compiled by Lawrence Keyes, President of O.C. Ministries, in his book, *The Last Age of Missions.* Some missionaries independently move out on their own; some missionaries work within very loosely structured organizations, but many come from structured agencies. In 1983, more than 600 third world mission agencies were run by national Christians. However, in his book Keyes uses the 1980 figure of 462 agencies to give a breakdown of who they are and where they are. Of these, 80 percent were listed as active; 192 agencies come from Asia, 104 from Africa, 56 from Latin America, 16 from Oceania, and 5 from Western countries (pp. 58-59).

Looking at the ten countries with the highest number of sending agencies, India is the leader with 66. Next in line are the Philippines, Brazil, Japan, Ghana, Korea, Kenya, Nigeria, Zaire, Indonesia, and Hong Kong (p. 60).

Are you surprised to see countries that are still receiving missionaries now on the sending list? Japan is still a major mission field with over 2,500 foreign missionaries there. Protestants make up only 1.2 percent of the population. At the same time, God is calling some from Japan to go out around the world.

Do you know which third world country leads in the number of missionaries sent? Nigeria is the leader with 2,500. Next is India with 2,277, and following are Ghana, Kenya, Burma, Oceania, Brazil, South Africa, the Philippines, and Korea (p. 68). These are moving out in cross-cultural ministries, sometimes from one people group to another and sometimes from one country to another.

Some of the missions are denominational and some are interdenominational; there seems to be an almost equal number in each. Some have been indigenous from their beginning; others have received encouragement from Western missions. They come from many different backgrounds and theological persuasions, but Keyes says that 77 percent of these non-Western missionaries are theologically evangelical (pp. 75-76).

One example of a third world mission is the Evangelical Missionary Society in Nigeria, which is sending out 500 missionaries throughout West Africa and in cross-cultural assignments in northern Nigeria. Harold Fuller, Deputy Director of SIM International, tells of this mission in his book, *Mission Church Dynamics* (William Carey Library). The Evangelical Churches of West Africa (ECWA) were founded by SIM missionaries, and the Evangelical Missionary Society (EMS) is the missionary arm of ECWA.

In Nigeria at an annual conference of SIM in 1949, three Yoruba young men were challenged by the need for missionaries in neighboring Dahomey (now Benin). They volunteered right there, and an offering was taken for their support. (One of those young men is now president of ECWA.) EMS missionaries have continued to go out from that time.

Finances for support were a challenge from the start. For the first 20 years, most of their missionaries had to farm to support their missionary work. The salary figure has increased through the years, but it still remains a sacrifice to go. The educational level of the missionaries has risen, and more educated people are joining the ranks all the time.

Like Western missionaries, the EMS missionaries have had to make cultural adjustments. Many of them come from animistic backgrounds, and their dress, their accent, their eating habits can be a stumbling block to the Muslims they are trying to reach. The missionaries have sometimes been accused of introducing Nigerian customs into countries like Benin, Ghana, and Chad.

But they have tried to fit into the culture even as they have moved from one people group to another in the same country. They have worked with the Maguzawa people of northern Nigeria, whose name means "runners" because their ancestors fled from the earlier Islamic invasion. The Maguzawa have a custom of holding a community feast to celebrate an important occasion. So, rather than announce new faith with individual baptism, the missionaries conducted group classes for new converts for baptism. At the time of baptism, the Christians then gathered from surrounding villages for the "feast of repentance." The Muslim neighbors watched this with interest because it was a culturally acceptable demonstration. The mission decided to have a separate Bible school for the Maguzawa converts so they would not be affected by the other cultures.

There are now 110 churches among these people. Large numbers have attended the Bible schools set up just for them, and graduates are now ready to go out to their own people (*SIM Now,* January-February 1983, p. 13).

It is encouraging to see how seriously ECWA takes this responsibility of reaching the yet unreached. At the Nigerian Congress on Evangelism, the challenge came to reach everyone in Nigeria for Christ in two years. The leaders calculated they would need 150 additional workers. They sent out 50 Bible school seniors to get started. Then they asked 100 churches to release their pastors for this work for one year.

"But how will we support these?" asked the overseers.

"Aren't they supported now?" was the reply. "Let the churches continue their salaries."

"But who will pastor the churches while they are away?" was the next question.

"The elders and deacons have the gifts of the Spirit," was the reply. "They can do the pastor's work while he's away. We've got to give this priority!" (Fuller, *Mission Church Dynamics,* p. 241)

An excellent lesson from the church in Nigeria in rearranging priorities for missions! Would we dare try this strategy here? Third world missions, like the Evangelical Missionary Society, are serious about reaching the unreached.

The call by leaders of emerging missions has been for cooperation with others from the third world for the sharing of ideas. They want their strategies to be indigenous and not foreign. They do not want to be a carbon copy of the Western mission structures.

## Their Distinct Advantages

The emerging missions have some distinct advantages. One of these is the community attitude that is generally characteristic of them. They find it easier to move into the other cultures that share this attitude, while the individualistic Western missionary has to learn it.

A good friend of ours, a Liberian on the ELWA radio staff, Margaret Traub, wrote for *Christianity Today,*

Community is the way of life for Africans in general. It is founded on man's need for each other and embodies a kindly awareness of others. . . . To an African unaccustomed to sophisticated city life, it is inconceivable that in some places a man can be stabbed to death on the street, and people hurry by as if they had not seen it—or that men and women can live together in apartment houses for years and never get to know each other. Such aloofness is completely foreign to the African nature and culture (20 July 1979, p. 10).

The message of the non-Western missionary is usually to the whole person. The message is that Jesus Christ not only saves from sin, but that He helps them in their work, with their crops, that He heals their diseases and defeats the invisible enemy. Keyes says that while John Wesley saw social reform follow his revivals, the modern third world missionaries take social reform with them (*The Last Age of Missions*, p. 43).

The non-Western missionary can work at much less cost. It may take $30,000 a year to keep a North American missionary family on the field, plus additional expenses for travel, children's education, and furlough. Third world missionaries usually live at levels closer to the people to whom they minister.

Many of the emerging mission workers live geographically and culturally closer to unreached peoples. Doug Miller of TEAM writes how missionaries from the Hatam tribe helped in reaching another tribe in Irian Jaya.

When Doug and his wife arrived in Dutch New Guinea (now Irian Jaya) in 1960, they heard the Moskona tribespeople described as cannibals who lived in trees. Other tribes spoke of them with fear, and no one ventured into Moskona land.

Doug was burdened for these people. He and his wife worked among the Hatam tribe, and he shared his burden with their church leaders. In 1971, Doug set out with several Hatam church leaders to contact the Moskonas. One of them could interpret the Moskona language.

It took three weeks to trek over treacherous land with sheer rock formations to climb. Sometimes they felt like ants crawling up and down acres of jagged coral formations, climbing hand over hand out on ledges where the drop-off went down hundreds of feet. But contact on this first trip was thwarted.

Next, Mission Aviation Fellowship planes helped with gift bombardments. Then one day they received word that the Moskona tribesmen wanted to meet them.

The second trip back ended when Doug fell and broke several ribs. Tribal warfare over the next three years kept them from trying again.

But finally in 1977 the way opened, and this time some of

the Hatam church leaders committed themselves to go as full-time missionaries to live among the Moskonas, and 76 Hatam churches were prepared to support them! This time five Hatam pastors and 17 other Hatam volunteers accompanied Doug Miller on the trip.

The Hatam missionaries had been working with the Moskona people less than two years when their first fetishes were burned. In September 1979 the first Moskona believer was baptized, and others followed. The Hatams were missionaries who were geographically and culturally closer to the Moskonas than were their Western counterparts ("Taking a Treasure to Tree-Dwellers," *Wherever,* TEAM, Winter 1980, pp. 5-7).

Third world missionaries also may be able to enter countries where Western missionaries are refused. They are able to work as tentmakers too.

## Particular Needs

But with their strengths, the non-Western missions are also aware of their particular needs. Stephen J. Akangbe, former president of the Evangelical Churches of West Africa and representative from Nigeria to the 1974 Lausanne International Congress of Evangelization, pointed out that in the area of theology there is need for stronger biblical understanding. Not only is liberal theology a threat, but there is also the threat of syncretism, the mixture of Christianity with traditional religions; and inconsistent Christian living is a deterrent (*Readings in Third World Missions,* ed. Marlin L. Nelson, William Carey Library, p. 176).

Other non-Western leaders have noted the need for more training in missiology. They say that missions as a subject has been left out of their curriculum in years past.

But third world missions are moving ahead in their own training programs, often at very practical levels. Some continue to use schools founded by Western missions, and others are developing their own.

The financial aspect of missions still poses a problem for the non-Western church, in spite of their ingenuity in doing the job.

Along with the lack of means for adequate support, there often is difficulty in maintaining contact between supporters and missionaries. This means that workers still may have to take care of themselves.

Like missions from the Western world, the emerging missions are concerned about the workers. One of their leaders, Rev. Theodore Williams, founding general secretary of the Indian Evangelical Mission and president of the World Evangelical Fellowship, wrote to missions in India:

"Our greatest need in missions today is the need of dedicated personnel. . . . Our greatest difficulty is to get quality workers." He went on to explain that with unemployment in India, people sometimes apply to missions just to get a job, without commitment to Christ or even being genuinely converted. "Recruitment through prayer rather than through advertisement seems to be the scriptural method." Most of the emerging missions feel that spirituality and servanthood should be the two major emphases of their missionary training ("Missionaries: What Kind?" *Frontier Fellowship,* WEF November '82).

## The Challenge Today

Missions around the world are encouraging one another in the great task. We are hearing other voices from the new enforcements as they now take part in world mission conferences. We are strengthened by these voices.

At the 1980 Edinburgh Conference on Frontier Missions, one-third of the mission agencies and one-third of the delegates were from non-Western missions. These are new voices in missions. Ralph D. Winter writes of the Edinburgh experience:

Three out of four of the plenary papers in the morning were assigned to third world mission leaders. And the entire conference obviously displayed the thrilling and exciting presence of these mature men of vision, disciplined and devoted, who had come from all over the world. I do not believe I will ever forget that conference. It almost seems my entire lifetime divides into two parts, before and after that conference ("The Explosion of New Missions within the Non-Western World," *Mission Frontiers,* January 1983, p. 7).

The call to missions of both worlds, or rather the whole world, is for encouragement and cooperation. A partnership should exist, no matter what the geographical or cultural distinctions.

In Africa, the truck is a means of transporting many people, and the overloaded truck is a common sight on the roadways. On the southern edge of the Sahara Desert in Niger Republic, an overloaded truck blew a tire and rolled over. About 40 passengers spilled out, and 33 of them were taken to Galmi Mission Hospital.

To their surprise, the surgeon was not a European as they expected, nor was he American nor African. He was Chinese. In the wards, a dark-haired Japanese nurse took care of them (*Africa Now,* SIM, August-October 1980, p. 2). There were probably Africans, Europeans, Americans, and Australians on the staff too.

This reminds us of the mission force around the world. People of many colors and backgrounds are carrying the banner for Jesus Christ to the ends of the earth. The body of Christ is international and interracial in nature.

The challenge is there, the potential is there, and the job of world evangelism is possible as the church around the world is mobilized.

# 10

# The Wall of Islam

"There is no god but Allah, and Muhammad is his prophet." These are words of the Islamic confession of faith, repeated by over 800 million people around the world. The followers of Islam, or Muslims as they are called, make up approximately 17 percent of the world's population. That's one of every six people. The Islamic religion, second only to Christianity in adherents, stands as a great obstacle to the advance of the Gospel of Jesus Christ around the world.

Early in our missionary career, we traveled to Nigeria and there visited the city of Kano at the edge of the Sahara Desert. The temperature soared well above 100 degrees. In the old part of the city, we saw the yellow mud-bricked compounds, one against another, surrounded by an outer wall that extends all around the old section of Kano. We stood outside the central mosque, the Muslim house of worship, and listened to the clear voice from the minaret calling all to noonday prayer. We watched thousands of white-robed men bow together, their foreheads touching the hot dry earth. We were reminded that the Muslim faith is like the wall around the old section of Kano, difficult to penetrate.

In North Africa, we sensed that we were outsiders as we walked the narrow streets of the markets of Casablanca. Missionaries are not allowed to work there.

Back in Liberia, we heard that the Muslim faith was spreading in West Africa. From our office window we could look out on the hospital patio and see the Muslim male patients spread their prayer rugs at the appointed times, face toward Mecca, and recite their prayers.

We sensed their submission to the will of Allah as these Muslims brought patients to the hospital. If a baby died because he was brought too late to the hospital with malnutrition, diarrhea, and dehydration—conditions which the doctor felt could have been avoided—the parents so easily seemed resigned to say, "Allah willed it." The name *Muslim* in Arabic means "one who submits," and so the followers of Islam submit to Allah, the God who determines destiny.

Other ancient world religions such as Hinduism and Buddhism present a challenge to Christianity's spread, but the newer religion of Islam moves out with its own aggressive missionary zeal. Today there is a resurgence of the Muslim faith around the world. Some say this is the fastest growing religion in the world.

We cannot help but be aware of the Muslim world as we see their people and customs on our television screens. We hear of the Middle East tensions, the age-old conflicts between Israel and the Arab countries that are Muslim. We see a new self-identity among the Muslims. Any religion which stands as such an obstacle in carrying out the Great Commission calls for a closer look.

## History

Islam had its beginning more recently than Christianity. Muhammad, the founder, was born in Arabia in the city of Mecca around A.D. 570. A major trade city, Mecca was also the location of an important house of worship—the Kaaba or House of Allah. The Arabic people trace their ancestry to Ishmael, the son of Abraham through Sarah's handmaid, Hagar, and their tradition says that Abraham and Ishmael rebuilt the Kaaba after a flood.

The people of Mecca recognized Allah as the supreme God,

but they also worshiped other deities. It is said that Muhammad searched for the true God, recognizing that the idols were false. While there were Jews and Christians in Arabia at that time, they evidently did little to make converts. Although the message of the Bible never was clear to Muhammad, in some Muslim teachings, ideas and stories seem to have been borrowed from Jewish and Christian Scriptures.

Tradition says that Muhammad used to go to a cave to meditate and seek God and that one night the Angel Gabriel appeared to him. Revelations continued to come to Muhammad through the years, always in the Arabic language, and these were recorded in the Koran, the Muslim holy book.

Muhammad considered himself to be a prophet of God. It was in 622 that he established a community of believers, and from this year the Muslims date their history. Muhammad and his followers moved out to conquer, sometimes with the sword. He became a political as well as religious leader. The Kaaba of Mecca became the center of Islam, and to this day Muslims face toward Mecca in their daily worship.

After the death of Muhammad in 632, the Arabs moved out with the zeal of a new religion to conquer other lands for Islam. They took Damascus, Antioch, Jerusalem, and moved on to Alexandria. They crossed North Africa and destroyed 900 Christian churches in their path! Spain fell to them in the early 700s. But they were stopped from going into France at the Battle of Tours in 732. Back they marched, toward Central Asia and into India.

Their conquest slowed for 500 years, but then the Ottoman Turks and Mongols of Central Asia picked up the cause, and Greece, the Balkans, and North India were targets. From India, Islam moved to Malaya, the East Indies, and the Philippine Islands (J. H. Kane, *Understanding Christian Missions,* Baker, p. 186).

Then Christendom moved with vengeance in the eleventh and twelfth centuries as the Crusaders marched to regain areas lost to Muslims, and ultimately to reach Jerusalem. During the march Christianity made no effort to convert, only to destroy.

J. Herbert Kane in *Understanding Christian Missions* says, "The Crusades were perhaps the greatest blunder ever made by the Christian church. . . . To this day Christianity's reputation for cruelty and revenge is a millstone around the neck of the Christian missionary in the Middle East" (p. 192).

In more recent centuries, some Muslim countries have felt the effects of colonization by so-called Christian countries. They have complained of exploitation. The events of history have made it more difficult to reach Muslims with the Gospel of Christ.

Itself a missionary movement, Islam is still on the march, most recently in East and West Africa and on into the Western world. Oil-rich countries have helped finance the building of mosques around the world, even in Rome, London, and Chicago! There are more than 50 nations that claim to be Islamic; some are Arab, but most are not. Islam is found in more than 150 countries. There is, however, diversity among the people and the countries. In Saudi Arabia, the only law is that of the Koran, and the conversion from Islam to the Christian faith is actually illegal. At the other end of the spectrum, Indonesia claims freedom of religion.

Christian witness to Muslims has always been very difficult. The most noted American missionary to the Muslim world was Samuel Zwemer who left for Arabia in 1890 and spent 60 years in the work. He was called "the Apostle to Islam."

Educational and medical institutions have been built in some countries to strengthen the witness for Christ, but through the years until the last decade, missionaries in Muslim areas have averaged only one convert per missionary life of service ("Islam—The Granite Wall," *Moody Monthly,* October 1979, p. 54).

One of the reasons why witness is difficult is that the Muslim world view is so different from that of the Christian, in many ways more similar to the world view of the Old Testament Hebrew. Islam encompasses every area of life; it is a total system with regulations for every aspect of life. Conformity is emphasized; the individual does not act independently. For the

Muslim, there is respect for the past; traditions are kept. In contrast, the modern Christian plans for the future, sets goals, and looks for change. While the family structure may be different than ours—the husband can have more than one wife—the family is still very important. The status of women may seem lower than in the Western world, but there is security in the regulations to which women conform. Islam deals in mysticism, placing emphasis on messages from dreams. This is contrary to the "scientific" Western world view (P. Parshall, *New Paths in Muslim Evangelism,* Baker, pp. 64-73).

## Doctrines

Just what are the tenets of the Muslim faith? Muslims say, "There is no god but Allah" (Allah means "the God" in Arabic). They confess that God is One. Christians also confess that God is One. But Muslims cannot understand this, for they interpret the Trinity of the Christian faith as three gods—God, Jesus, and Mary. They cannot comprehend the Three in One of the Trinity. Both faiths see God as the Creator, but the Koran does not teach that He is a personal, loving Father or that He has revealed Himself in the person of Jesus Christ, as the New Testament says.

The Christian finds Muslims unreceptive to answers from the Bible. Muslims point to the text of what they believe to be a newer revelation, one greater than any preceding ones, the Koran. Other revelations have been given, they concede, and four have been preserved—the Law of Moses, the Psalms of David, the Gospels of Jesus, and the Koran—but they claim that Jews and Christians have tampered with the Old and New Testaments and have made changes. Only the Koran is the final authority, they reason.

Prophets have been sent by Allah. The great prophets that Muslims name are Adam, Noah, Abraham, Moses, Jesus, and Muhammad. But Muhammad was the greatest, and there will be no other prophet. Angels have an important place in their faith, but genies also carry out good and evil.

The Koran pictures a final judgment day, with Paradise, and

plenty of food, drink, and sensual pleasures waiting for those who have confessed Allah and whose good deeds outnumber the bad. Hell awaits those whose bad deeds have weighted the balance.

Islam says it's possible to save oneself by good deeds, in contrast to Christianity which says salvation comes only by faith in God's Son who died for sinners. Therefore, Muslims have a system of do's and don'ts and good deeds to work their way to Paradise. Five religious duties referred to as the Pillars of Faith are the most important.

A true Muslim says, "There is no god but Allah, and Muhammad is the apostle of Allah." This is the Witness, the first pillar required of believers. The second pillar is Worship, and Muslims are often identified by their ritual of prayer five times a day as they turn to face Mecca. Fasting is another duty, and the month of Ramadan is set aside for this. Almsgiving is another pillar.

We sensed the religious fervor building up in Liberian friends who were making their first pilgrimage to Mecca. A pilgrimage to Mecca at least once during a lifetime is the fifth pillar. Thousands converge on this city in the desert of Arabia, the birthplace of Muhammad, for special Muslim rituals during the twelfth month of the Muslim calendar. From around the world they arrive by planes, buses, ships, caravans, and even on foot, often enduring great hardships to fulfill their required duty.

Do we better understand why it is hard to witness to Muslims? There is the solidarity of a community of believers, a lifestyle that permeates every area. Another way of salvation is offered. They have another scripture. And there is a political barrier.

But the bottom line is their conflict with the person of Jesus Christ. What do Muslims think of Jesus? They say He performed miracles and was sinless, but was nothing more than a good prophet, and that Muhammad was greater. They cannot accept the deity of Jesus Christ. They argue that it was impossible for God to have a wife; this would be blasphemous, they say.

Neither did Jesus die on the cross. They believe a prophet of God could never come to such an end! They teach that at the last minute God sent a substitute, and Jesus was raptured away. Someone else died on the cross instead!

In Liberia the Mandingo people are Muslim, and a major effort is being made to minister to them. Mandingo radio broadcasts have paved the way, and friendships are being made. Dr. Ed and Nancy Manring wrote in their prayer letter of a Mandingo woman who frequently came to the ELWA Hospital, often bringing others with her. Satta was friendly to the staff, and she listened politely as they spoke to her of Jesus.

One day she sat down in Dr. Manring's office to talk. Satta was upset because her husband had taken a third wife. She was interested in the Gospel, but she said that if she ever became a Christian, she would be put out of her family. She would lose her children to other family members, and she would have no friends.

Evidently Satta had been sharing what she had learned about Jesus, because she said, "My people tell me the man who died on the cross was not Jesus—it was His friend. They tell me God has no son. God would never lie with a woman."

Satta went on to say that the thing that convinced her most about the truth of Christ was the behavior of believers. In Liberian English, she said, "Doctor, I want to be a Christian, but I just can't able."

That statement reflects the conflict between the Muslim faith and Christianity, the conflict over the person of Jesus Christ. The Muslim does not realize that Jesus Christ is the Saviour from sin, that Jesus Christ conquered death, and that only through Him can they have eternal life. They do not know the Good News!

To convert to Christianity is to be apostate, and their Law of Apostasy says, "He who departs from Islam being disobedient to God and His apostle, let him be cut off or crucified or destroyed from this earth." In some countries this means that a close family member is responsible to kill the convert to Christianity. In other places less fanatical, it means harassment, being cut off from family and friends.

Looking at the history of mission work among the Muslims is not encouraging. Here and there are a few conversions, but it remains a very difficult task. But have we too easily accepted the notion that there will always be just a few converts? Does that mean that we should give up? Doesn't the Great Commission still include all people everywhere?

Missions that are serious about the task of reaching Muslims for Christ are pooling resources, asking questions of one another, again examining their strategies. If our methods have yielded so little fruit in the past, they ask, shouldn't we look for new ways?

When the North American Conference on Muslim Evangelism convened in 1978, W. Stanley Mooneyham of World Vision spoke of another conference which Samuel Zwemer organized in 1906. He said, "That was almost 70 cultural light-years ago, and there have been enormous changes. These times cry for a new understanding and new approaches" (Don M. McCurry, ed., *The Gospel and Islam:* A 1978 Compendium MARC, p. 23).

## Contextualization

One thing that mission leaders have noted is that the Muslim world has seen little of the Christian church within its own culture, a culture that is unique and so important to them. In many areas, Christian churches are made up of congregations of foreigners who live within the country and who never were Muslims. Few churches are formed of actual Muslim converts. Instead of seeing the church alive within their own people, they still recall the brutal Crusades of the past, the cruelties. They see the materialism of the West in people they assume are Christians. They hear of the moral degeneration in "Christian" countries. From their perspective, Christianity doesn't offer them anything.

The Christian church that is already established is structured after the Western pattern. Phil Parshall, missionary to Bangladesh with International Christian Fellowship, raises the question: How would an American feel if, in a small town in the

Bible Belt, an orthodox Egyptian Muslim priest with a long black beard and dressed in a flowing white robe moved into a mansion and began to propagate Islam? If he continued to set up the patterns of worship in every way strange to the community, how popular would he be with the local population? (Phil Parshall, *New Paths in Muslim Evangelism*, Baker, p. 234)

Looking at it from the other side of the world, from the Muslim perspective, Phil Parshall's teenage daughter Lindy wrote a story called "The Valley of Decision," which we have her permission to tell. Born in Bangladesh, she lived most of her life in that country, and understands the culture.

Lindy wrote of Akbar Khan who stood on the corner near the foreign church in a Muslim land and watched, curious as people walked through the gate to the majestic building, dressed in their best clothes. He saw the high walls with the barbed wire to keep out the beggar kids. He looked up at the cross on top of the building and thought, "How awful!" It reminded him of the stories of the Crusaders who had carried crosses.

Akbar felt strange as he followed the others toward the building. It was Sunday, and he normally went to worship on Friday. He walked past the missionary's nice house and noted the luxury of an electric fan that only the banker or other high-class people had in his village. He recalled how everyone spoke of the white man who always wore clean suits and had plenty of them. The missionary had supplied the money for the church building, and they thought he probably still had a lot of money left.

Akbar unbuckled his sandals and left them outside as he entered, but he noticed that not many had done so. "How repulsive," he thought. He looked around and saw new chairs. How different from the mosque where he sat on the floor! It was unusual to see women there too.

In her story, Lindy Parshall vividly portrays the conflicts in the mind of this Muslim man as he sees so many things that offend his way of life. The songs are of strange melody, not the chants he is used to. The people don't change positions when they pray; they just sit in their chairs. He thinks, "How different is this religion!"

That night Akbar again stands in front of the electrically lit church and watches people go in. But he also sees the mosque in the distance lit with candles, and he turns and slowly walks down the dusty road to the mosque.

Lindy Parshall reminds us of the Apostle Paul's methods:

> And to the Jews I became as a Jew, that I might gain the Jews, to them that are under the law, as under the law, that I might gain them that are under the law. . . . I am made all things to all men, that I might by all means save some (1 Cor. 9:20, 22, KJV).

Leaders in Muslim evangelism are asking, "Have our methods gotten in the way of our message?" They are looking at contextualization for help, presenting the Gospel within the context of the community, using methods familiar to the people, without sacrificing the message.

Phil Parshall describes one such experiment going on in a Muslim country which he gives the fictitious name of Lombaro. The witness begins in areas of the familiar, such as with Old Testament stories also found in the Koran. The missionaries rent simple homes and wear the clothing of the people. Some of the men have full beards like the Muslim religious leaders. They eat the food of the Muslims, and fit into the time schedule of the community.

At worship, shoes are left at the door. The practices of prayer are similar to the Muslim habits. The music is Muslim in tune and chants are used. Many adaptations have been made, and even the word *Christian* is avoided because of the negative historical connotations. Instead, believers are called Followers of Isa (Jesus) (*New Paths in Muslim Evangelism,* pp. 21-27).

The church is tied into the culture without sacrificing the message of the Gospel of Christ. The result is that there are many more converts in Lombaro, according to Parshall. Few were won by the missionaries, but the Muslim converts began witnessing from the day of conversion. The church is made up entirely of those who were formerly Muslims.

Finding new ways to make the Gospel relevant to people in their own culture, without compromising the message, is the thrust of missions to Muslims. This presents a tremendous challenge.

Radio is still an effective means to penetrate behind the closed doors where missionaries cannot go. Letters from listeners are filled with questions. There are those who become followers of Jesus, and correspondence courses are sent out for Bible study. But again, the hours of broadcasting or the printing of literature can be a waste unless it is relevant to these special people.

Tentmakers go to closed countries as businessmen, advisers, technicians, engineers, geologists, agriculturists, nurses, doctors, and others. A great responsibility rests on these who take the opportunity not only to live among the people but to understand them, to love them, and to look for unique ways to share Jesus Christ with them.

## Western Muslims

But there is a new opportunity right in our own country! We are seeing more people of the Muslim faith coming to North America than ever before. There are the businessmen and the tourists, many from lands recently made oil-rich. There are diplomatic personnel. But thousands are in the student population. Many of these students are not especially religious in their thinking. While they are away from the traditional Muslim community pressures, they may be ready to consider the claims of Christianity.

We visited with the Mission Coordinator of Park Street Church in Boston, Betty Vetterlein, and talked with her about their exciting program for international students. We asked her, "Do you really see converts from the Muslim faith?"

And she answered, "Oh, yes, we do!"

A beautiful young woman from Iran was a bridesmaid at a wedding we recently attended. The bride was Ruthie Atkinson, daughter of Dr. Herb and Freida Atkinson who served many years in the Congo with Africa Inland Mission and now are in Bob's medical group.

When we were introduced to Ruthie's friend, it was easy to recognize the strikingly beautiful features of her Middle East background. We were told that she was working on her Ph.D. in Immunology in Chicago. It was obvious that she was a very intelligent young woman. We were curious about her background. Was she Muslim?

Ruthie told us that her friend had become a Christian since coming to this country. She was from a Muslim background, though she had not been strong in her faith.

Later we visited with the Iranian student and she shared more about herself. She said, "I was really turned off at first by the Christian students I met. They came on too strong! They said that I had to know Jesus Christ!

"I knew they meant well as they told me about all those people who had accepted Christ and how their lives had been changed—drug addicts and the like—but I thought, *That's fine for them, but I'm basically a nice person, so that's not for me."*

We asked her about her Muslim background. She told us that while the culture, the traditions, the world views of the Muslims had definitely held a strong influence on her, she was at the point in her own life where she really didn't think that God existed.

She met Ruthie at a Christian concert, and there became acquainted with more Christians. As friendships grew, she enjoyed the talks about all kinds of subjects, the exchange of ideas, the intellectual stimulation. She said, "Sometimes these sessions lasted until three in the morning, but we always ended talking about Jesus Christ."

She became curious about the basic reason for Christianity. She read books like Josh McDowell's *Evidence That Demands a Verdict,* and C.S. Lewis' *Mere Christianity.* She bought more books.

Then she started reading the New Testament, and before she got through the four Gospels, she decided, "I had to say yes to Jesus Christ simply because I couldn't say no. It was God who put the desire within me to know Him." From Iran to Chicago to faith in Christ.

Mission organizations that work abroad, but have headquarters here, are adjusting their strategy to include Muslims right here. The Southern Baptist Convention has several Arab churches that minister to immigrants, many of them Muslims. International Students, Inc., includes the Muslim students as a special group to reach (*The Gospel and Islam:* Compendium, p. 233).

Is the wall that has been so hard to penetrate with the Gospel cracking in some places? Have you read of any openings? Some predict that as Muslim nations become more involved politically with the rest of the world, there may be a softening of resistance. What about those people who have become followers of Jesus Christ while in the West; when they return to their own countries, will they take the Gospel to their Muslim relatives and friends? How many secret believers are behind the wall as they have heard the Gospel over radio or through literature? Will we hear more of them? Will we see more churches formed of Muslim converts?

The task remains difficult. It always has been. Samuel Zwemer compared it to mountain climbing, as one rarely sees the summit as he climbs along the dangerous path. "But," he said, "the sight of the summit—the goal—makes the hardships worth the struggle."

Samuel Zwemer, one who knew that struggle all too well as he was in Muslim work for 60 years, continued, "The evangelization of the Muslim world is a task so great, so difficult, so discouraging at times that only the upward look can reassure the climbers" (*The Gospel and Islam:* Compendium, p. 36).

Can we, more informed about the people of the Muslim world, somehow join in that climb? Perhaps prayer, another upward look, is our first step.

# 11

# Interference from the Communist Voice

It was at a beautiful old castle in the Alps in Europe that we first met them. They were gathered at a field conference for the Slavic Gospel Association. A cool rain was falling that first evening as we climbed the steps and walked down the narrow corridors to the stark room that would be the meeting place that week. Peter Deyneka, Jr., an old friend from Wheaton College days and now General Director of SGA, had invited Bob to speak to the Christian workers on interpersonal relationships.

Bob said, "As I looked at that group that first evening I wondered, 'What do I have to tell them about relationships?' "

These were workers in Eastern Europe who had gathered for the field conference. Some of them were missionaries who had long been going in and out of Communist countries to assist the church there. There were Christian workers who had come from their native Communist countries, no doubt under some other pretext, but nonetheless looking for encouragement through the conference. There were radio broadcasters from the studios in Monte Carlo. There were workers from the refugee camps of Western Europe. There were students from the West who had come to help deliver literature across the barbed-wire borders, as tourists, to eastern European countries. There was a vehicle maintenance worker who kept the vans in good order.

Bob said, "I felt the warmth of their greetings as they embraced. I looked into the eyes of a suffering church, at people who were realistically facing an ideology that I had not had to confront." The thought troubled him. "Who was I to talk to them about interpersonal relationships? I would have failed had I not shared from the Word of God, invariably practical in all situations."

One thing this diverse group had in common was their work with people under the control of an ideology which is the greatest challenge to Christianity since the invasion of Muslim forces into North Africa in the seventh century! Karl Marx, German philosopher and journalist who later lived in England, introduced this ideology in the late nineteenth century. With Friedrich Engels he coauthored the *Communist Manifesto,* a statement of the theories that became known to the world as Marxism.

It was the twentieth century before Communism became a threat to Christianity when, following the Revolution of 1917, Russia embraced this ideology under the leadership of Lenin. Communism has continued to spread around the world, with two powers—Russia and China—the leaders today. From East Europe and Asia, the movement has also gone into third world countries, some of these borderline Communist. Almost 50 percent of the world's people are living under Communism. Marxism has been especially appealing to the oppressed and the idealistic, as it has promised a better world with economic wealth distributed equitably.

Marxism is an atheistic ideology. It is an all-encompassing view of the world as only material, with no place for spiritual values. Man, matter, and nature are the ultimate realities. Marxists claim that when the economic base is put in the right order, with everything shared by the people, society will function properly. Communists admit that their ultimate goal has not yet been reached, but they say that the present system is a part of the process toward ultimate Communism.

Religion is viewed as a weakness which hinders the advance of this ideology. Karl Marx said, "Religion is the opiate of the people." He thought religion would just wither away as people experienced Communism. Lenin went further. He thought religion had to be openly combated. Stalin said, "We are conducting and we will conduct a campaign against religious prejudices." Mao said, "It is necessary to eradicate in the people the backward and stupid superstition of religion."

However, the degree of opposition to religion varies from country to country. For example, in Poland where over 90 percent of the population is Roman Catholic, there is limited religious freedom, while in Albania, religion has been declared illegal. But the goal of true Communism is to eliminate religion.

Constitutions of most Communist countries include guarantees of religious freedom. But the Communist party, which is avowedly opposed to religion, is the leading and guiding force and so the final authority rests there.

The church is viewed as an adversary. But here the Communists have a problem! Most Communist countries wish to protect their image to the world and demonstrate that freedoms do exist within their borders. The result is that the Communists often go to great lengths to not appear to be doing what they are doing—suppressing religion.

## Troubles for the Church

In Communist countries, the Christian church works around restrictions, oppression, and Marxist indoctrination. In the Soviet Union, for example, restrictions are used to control the church. To be officially recognized, churches must be registered by the Soviet government. There are restrictions on the number of churches in each area. The church is to be contained within the four walls and is not to be involved in social concerns. Because religious education is not viewed as scientific, youth under 18 are not permitted to receive organized religious instruction. There are no officially sanctioned Sunday Schools. Communist leaders often attempt to work through the church leadership, making it appear that church leaders are responsible for the decisions, and not the Communist party. Regulations are sometimes directed to choke the life of the church through the church's own leaders. There are no Protestant Bible schools or seminaries in Russia. Printing of Christian literature is under the control of the government.

Oppression of the individual believer is another way to suppress religion. It may seem subtle, but Christians do not usually get promoted in their jobs. They are often harassed—problems even created—to make them look bad. Only those who belong to the party are recommended for certain studies at the University. Christians can be under surveillance. Houses may be searched, and interrogations usually follow. For some it may mean prison. Children are sometimes removed from families because of the threat of "harmful" Christian teaching. At times psychiatry is used as a means to claim that Christians are mentally ill.

Pastors are a special group for harassment. Russian Baptist Pastor Dmitrii Miniakov is one of these. His story is told in the book, *A Song in Siberia,* by Anita and Peter Deyneka, Jr. (Cook). He represents those whose message troubles Communists. His church in Siberia was padlocked, and the house where the believers then met for worship was bulldozed to the ground. He was imprisoned for "organizing harmful religious meetings." Three times he served prison sentences in Siberia. In prison he suffered from severe asthma. All he would have needed to do was to renounce his faith. He was carried from prison on a stretcher.

Dmitrii and his family moved from Siberia to the Baltic States, but found no greater freedom there. He was forced into hiding to elude the KGB. When his wife died in 1980, he did not dare to attend her funeral because he was a fugitive. He had to visit her grave secretly.

In 1981, Dmitrii, then 59, was again arrested, and the latest report is that he is suffering from tuberculosis in prison. His five children continue to stand steadfast in the faith.

Pastors of registered churches whose message makes the government uncomfortable are often sent to out-of-the-way places to minister.

But the church is not destroyed! In fact, the Communists have cause for alarm because of the increased interest in religion. Even the youth who have been totally immersed in an atheistic environment are asking questions. They are disillusioned because Communism has not brought fulfillment. The Soviet press has noted with concern a revival of religion among the youth. The believers no longer conform to the old Soviet stereotype of an uneducated old woman who is outside the mainstream of the system! Brezhnev was concerned too, and in the early 1980s called for 22 special Marxist training schools to be launched to prepare "missionaries" for atheism!

There is the tactic of indoctrination. Soviet citizens are bombarded with Communist ideology. Beginning in nursery schools the children sing:

> Lenin is always alive:
> Lenin is always with us:
> In sorrow, in home, in joy,
> Lenin is in our thoughts.
> In each happy day,
> Lenin is in you and me.

Through the entire educational system, atheism is promoted. The rest of society is bombarded with drama, lectures, films, TV programs, and posters on atheism. The presses roll out atheistic literature.

How is the church reacting to restrictions, oppression, and indoctrination? It is impossible to generalize from one country to another, but usually the response comes in these ways:

• Some accept the restrictions and controls as inevitable, and try to exist within the structure as registered churches.

• Some choose to be unregistered, to avoid the interference of authorities. Many of these are house churches.

• Some try to fight through the legal system to defend their rights of separation from the state.

It is hard for us to make any judgments when we don't live under those conditions. The believers there must seek God's guidance as to how the church is to function.

## How Can Missions Help?

What is the role of missions in the Communist world? The notion that the door is closed is a misconception. While it is true that the traditional missionary can no longer go into most Communist countries, there still are ways to go as tentmakers, students, and tourists. Media ministries, such as radio and literature, are especially effective in missions to Communist countries.

If we ask the church there, "What do you need?" their first answer probably would be, "Literature." The priority would be Bibles. Secret presses in the Soviet Union have begun printing some Bibles because the need is so great. No Bibles or Christian books can be found in bookstores in the USSR. There is also a need for books on subjects like marriage and family life, and other books that show the validity of the Christian faith to counteract atheistic philosophy. Children's literature is needed too.

After Western missions print literature, it has to be moved across the borders. Some missions carefully conceal the material in an effort to smuggle it across, while others just take it, aware that if it is seen, it may be confiscated. If a carrier is stopped, interrogations can last many hours. There is the threat of imprisonment for bringing in literature that authorities view as contrary to Communist teaching.

When we were in Europe, we met a number of students who were involved in delivering literature as tourists. One described the apprehension that accompanies the task:

"At the border there's a great barrier of steel barbed wire and concrete, antitank ditches, and machine gun posts. There is only one way you can penetrate that barrier, and that's by the prayers of the folks back home, and by the Lord moving into the situation and working a miracle.

"We arrived at this difficult frontier late one night. Our vehicle was loaded with literature. We took our place in line. I switched off the ignition and we waited. The guards thoroughly searched the two vehicles in front of us. We watched as one was refused entrance, and the other was allowed to pass through the barricade.

"Now it was our turn to move to the frontier. I switched on the ignition, and nothing happened. After some time the border guard got impatient because we were blocking the way. I kept trying to start the engine, but the battery seemed dead.

"And then a wonderful thing happened. I'm sure that the Lord was right there with us. The barricade was raised so that the road was cleared. Two soldiers went to the back of our vehicle, and as the border guard yelled instructions, they pushed our car unsearched over the border! Then they stepped back, saluted us very smartly, and said, 'Good night!' We were on our way!"

The student added, "They didn't know it, but those two soldiers had pushed the Word of God into their own country!"

Precise instructions are given to find the Christian contacts for literature delivery, but it's not always easy. "Parking a distance away so not to draw attention," another student recalled, "we walked up the dark, deserted dirt path and turned onto the street where we would meet our contact. It seemed that every house had a barking dog! We imagined the people peering out of their curtained windows, and then telephoning the 'polezei' to inform them of the suspicious Western strangers.

"Our instructions were to look for the multistory house along the path on the right. We looked closely and saw not one, but two houses fitting that description! The house number on the fence was between the two houses. We became nervous. What should we do?

"In the end, we walked down the middle driveway, and a car drove in behind us. The Lord again proved faithful, for the man in the car was our contact, and he quietly invited us in."

Story after story recount the Lord's protection and direction in these ventures.

The training of pastors and Christian workers is another area where the church asks for help. As Christian workers from the West go into these countries as visitors, they can often meet with the Christians and conduct short seminars. One such worker says, "I found out later that a pastor who had been at the seminars used the same material to lead a conference for more than 50 pastors the next summer."

Theological Education by Extension (TEE) is an effective teaching tool for the church in Communist lands. Textbooks and workbooks brought in make it possible for pastors to study in their own homes. Seminary studies are broadcast over missionary radio stations.

Radio is a very powerful means for communicating the Gospel to Communist countries. Cut off from the news of the outside world, many listen to shortwave radio. A 28-year-old laborer from a city in the USSR wrote to HCJB in Quito, Ecuador: "Back in my youth I became fascinated by philosophy. I was interested in Marxism, existentialism, and other philosophical systems. But these philosophies did not satisfy me as I sought answers to life. I became interested in religion and read a stack of religious books published by our government from an atheistic perspective. I got little information.

"The main source of my knowledge of the Christian faith came from radio broadcasts. As a result, I have been a believer in our Lord Jesus Christ for several years." He asked for a Bible because he had not been able to find one.

Many are converted through Christian broadcasts. Those who work in positions where they will lose their job if they attend a church consider radio their church and their Bible.

The work of missions reaches to emigrants held at transit points. Bored and often discouraged, they welcome friendships. Missions also look for pockets of immigrants in North America as they come from Communist lands.

But many Christians want to stay in the Communist lands because they truly love their countries. "This is home," they say. Proud of their ethnic heritage, they want to live and work for Christ where they are.

## What Can We Learn?
What can we learn from this suffering church? An East European Christian scientist working in the Soviet Union says he is officially forbidden to discuss Christianity in his work. But he

secretly meets with some colleagues for Bible study. He told Peter Deyneka, Jr., "Communism, with the suffering it has brought to believers, has swept away corrupt and lukewarm Christianity in our country. Communism has created a vacuum which can only be filled with vital Christianity. And this is what is happening" (Anita and Peter Deyneka, Jr., "A Salvation of Suffering," *Christianity Today*, 16 July 1982, p. 21).

Suffering has increased the faith of the Christians. Dmitri Dudko, Russian Orthodox priest imprisoned for his ministry, said, "Faith withers on earthly well-being; and in the West there's well-being, so faith is weaker there" (*Ibid.*, p. 20).

In Communist lands, there is a witnessing church, ingenious in arranging situations for sharing. And it is a praying church. All over Russia there are Christians who designate Friday as a day of prayer—for their children, for Christians in prison, for Christian radio broadcasts, for those who bring in literature. "But," Deyneka says, "on some Fridays they pray for the church in the West—for you and me."

That really makes us stop and think! How can we help the church there? Are we even seriously praying for the church behind the Iron Curtain? The Slavic Gospel Association, with headquarters in Wheaton, Illinois, has a Strategic Prayer Program for Russia, to involve people who want to pray.

"It's a David and Jonathan relationship," an Eastern European Christian pointed out to Deyneka. "Jonathan had all the luxuries, material blessings, and security; David had little but his faith, and he had to struggle to stay alive, as King Saul pursued him. But even with different backgrounds, they cared for one another. While Jonathan was secure and David on the run, Jonathan never stopped helping David and never forgot him. Jonathan took on David's problems as his own." Do we realize we are a part of this relationship?

## On the Other Side of the Communist World

There is another story to be told of the church in Communist China. At the close of the 1970s, China with its one billion people began to open up to the outside world. We were teaching a Sunday School class on missions when Chinese-American friends shared with us a taped message from a veteran missionary who had just been into China. We sat spellbound, as if we were walking with him back across the bridge into China. We laughed and cried as he related what he experienced on his first trip back. We have his permission to share some of his experiences with you.

He told of his friend from Hong Kong who visited one of the recently opened, packed-out churches. People stood in line for hours to get in. The visitor was given a mimeographed song sheet as he entered. Standing next to him, in their beautifully pressed white blouses and blue slacks, with their hair in pigtails, were two girls between 18 and 21 years of age. The pastor announced the hymn, "Holy, Holy, Holy," and this friend thought he better share his song sheet with the girls. But before he could get it out of his pocket, they were already singing—

Holy, Holy Holy, Lord God Almighty,
Early in the morning, our songs shall rise to Thee.

He said, "They sang every verse of the hymn, looking toward heaven. It was like standing beside angels as they sang. Tears ran down the girls' faces as they worshiped the Lord Jesus Christ in that church."

That might not seem so impressive to us, but he reminded us that those same girls lived through the Cultural Revolution. They had watched Christians march by with signs that said, "I am a monster," "I am a devil," "I am a fool," "Spit on me," "I am on my way to jail." All these years the girls had heard about Christians being persecuted. They knew that things could change in government any time, and that they also could be put in jail. This visiting Christian watched as the young ladies got down on their knees and cried in gratitude for the opportunity to worship God in public.

In our Sunday School class, we felt like cheering, "The church is alive in China!" For years we had heard nothing of the church there, and actually wondered if it had died out.

When the Communists took over in 1949, China was the largest Protestant mission field with over 6,000 missionaries. There were an estimated 1.8 million baptized believers. Today we hear of an estimated 25 million Christians in China! The church is alive!

China is an ancient culture reaching back more than 4,000 years. During the dynasties, there was little contact with the outside world. As trade was established and outside contacts made, missionaries came to China. But the Gospel was viewed as foreign.

Following World War I, a peasant revolution brought an end to dynasties. Missionary work was encouraged. The Japanese invasion during World War II was followed by struggles and in 1949 by the Communist takeover.

The church was brought under the control of the Communist government through the pro-government Chinese Christian Three-Self Patriotic Movement (self-government, self-support, and self-propagation). The number of churches was drastically cut. Christianity was again considered a foreign influence, and the missionaries were sent home. Mission institutions were closed, and atheistic indoctrination followed. Many Christians were imprisoned, especially those who had been associated with foreign agencies.

Things turned even worse in 1966 with the Cultural Revolution, when all churches were closed and thousands were imprisoned. Christianity was included in the "four olds" to be destroyed—old ideology, old customs, old habits, old culture.

But with the death of Mao in 1976, there came a new openness to the world and a release of pressure on religion.

While the Chinese church is more visible now, it is still under the control of the government and lives with many restrictions. The Protestant Three-Self Patriotic movement and the Catholic Patriotic Association have been restored as the official voices of the churches. More churches have been opened, and many are filled, some with more than one service. Church attendance is still regarded by the Communist party as foolish and superstitious.

The strength of the church is also seen in another phenomenon, the House Church movement, that existed during the years when the institutionalized church was closed. Very small groups, often just families, met secretly in those years. Today it is estimated that some 40,000 such groups meet in every province and practically every major village. The freedom to meet will depend on local officials; the groups vary in size from a very small house meeting to as high as 2,000 gathering in a park!

Reports say that these churches are the Book of Acts in action. The tape we listened to told of a missionary going to visit China. A Chinese woman in Hong Kong asked him to take a Bible to her son who was a hard-core Communist.

When the missionary arrived at the village where the son lived, he met some Christians who told him, "Don't go near that man. He will get you into all kinds of trouble." They told him the son was a doctor at the local hospital.

The missionary was afraid to go, but he knew he had to. He kept the Bible all wrapped up so no one could see it. When he went to the home, the son met him at the door and said, "Please come in, I want to speak to you." But the missionary said, "I don't need to. I just want to give you this gift from your mother." But the man insisted, "Come in."

The missionary entered but thought he was in a trap. The man then said, "Sit down. I want to tell you something."

Then he told the missionary this story: "Six weeks ago I was on duty at the emergency ward. That night an accident victim was brought in. A large boulder had fallen on her and she was crushed. There was no hope."

He X-rayed her and found that all her ribs were broken and her lung was pierced.

As they were putting her on a bed, this doctor heard her groan. He listened as she said, "Jesus, rescue me, Jesus, save me." He told the nurse, "This lady will be dead by morning," and he went home.

When he came back to the hospital the next morning, the lady was sitting on the edge of her bed eating her breakfast.

He walked over and asked, "What are you doing?" She said, "I am eating breakfast!"

He went over the nurse and said, "What is that lady doing?" The nurse said, "She is eating her breakfast!" But not only was she eating her breakfast, she had gone around the ward helping feed the others and telling them about Jesus!

He again X-rayed the woman, and found that all her bones were healed. He went back to his house, got down on his knees, and said, "I do not know who Jesus is, but I must believe in Him. He is real."

He and the missionary discussed God's Word for three hours. Then the doctor said, "Take me out and baptize me."

The missionary said, "I don't dare, I'll get into trouble."

The doctor said, "Don't worry, I'm the guy who *gives* the trouble, not the guy who gets in trouble." And the missionary baptized him. The people who told us this story said they have a file full of similar incidents.

We are thrilled to know that God is at work in China. Certainly there still are many tensions. It is possible that the age of the Western missionary working there is a thing of the past, that God may choose other means. But there are ways to be of help and encouragement.

There is a need for church leadership training, just as in other Communist lands. Printing presses put out a limited supply of Bibles, and there is need for many more and for other Christian literature. Radio broadcasts are also an effective way of helping.

There are opportunities for Christians to visit China. Businessmen, doctors, engineers, and other experts are going in on exchange programs. This means that many Chinese are also able to come to Western countries.

Some Chinese people are involved in exchanges with non-Western countries. Dr. Frank Young, missionary doctor in Liberia, writes:

Just down the road from ELWA the Chinese are building a stadium. It is not unusual to have four or five of these men strolling around ELWA on a Sunday afternoon, or coming to the hospital for treatment. What is unusual is that God has only recently placed in our midst one Chinese girl from New York, and our first East Asian career missionary, a Chinese man from Hong Kong. They are busily seizing opportunities to speak with these folks.

It is especially encouraging to hear of Chinese Christians all around the world who are getting involved in reaching their brothers and sisters in China. Certainly the Lord can use them better than anyone else in this outreach. Strategic ministries such as the Christian Nationals Evangelism Commission and the Chinese Church Research Center are working in this area.

We wait expectantly to learn more about the church in China. We watch and we pray. Sister Claire, the lovely Christian from China, said, "We believe the second coming of Christ is near. But before He comes, there are still nearly one billion Chinese who have never heard of Jesus Christ. So I think He will delay until they hear, and then He will come.

"Now we see that this is the time of harvest, but we are short of the workers. So my prayer is this: let all the real Christians who love the Lord pray for China. We believe because this door has been opened by the Lord Himself, He Himself is going to finish the salvation planning for China!"

# 12

# The Sending Church

Jesus told the 72 workers whom He was sending out, "The harvest is plentiful, but the workers are few. Ask the Lord of the harvest, therefore, to send workers into His harvest field" (Luke 10:2). It is God who sends.

But just as God uses people to take the message, He also uses people to send others out. In Acts 13 we read where the church at Antioch sent out Paul and Barnabas, following the instructions of the Holy Spirit. Even though there still was much that these very gifted men could have done right there in Antioch, the church sent them off to Europe and Asia Minor. The local church became a sending church according to God's plan for carrying out His mission.

## The Importance of Vision
The sending church needs vision—a world vision. Jesus told His disciples, "Open your eyes and look at the fields! They are ripe for harvest" (John 4:35). We are sure that their eyes weren't really closed, but evidently they needed an adjustment in vision.

We joke in our family about what all we've been through for Bob's vision. Just before leaving for Liberia in 1962, an optometrist friend in our church wanted to give Bob his first contact lenses. Bob had worn glasses since the seventh grade and really wasn't that convinced about contacts. But our friend assured him that they would be invaluable in the tropics where his regular glasses would steam up and slip down over the mask while he was doing surgery.

So Bob tried them, and to his amazement and the credit of an excellent fitting, he got used to them right away. He has worn contacts since then. He has had a few problems though, not with the fit but with losing them in strange places. This has been an embarrassment to Bob, and the family has often had to come to the rescue in the search.

About a year ago Bob thought the contacts were giving him some trouble with his vision. So he drove the four hours to Midland, Michigan only to be told that he shouldn't wear the right lens on the left eye, and vice versa! It didn't take long to correct that!

Vision is so important! We have problems if we are nearsighted and problems if we are farsighted. When Jesus told the disciples to look at the fields, their vision had to include the section of the field right beside them and the far-distant corners. To see the whitened grain in need of harvest, their vision had to adjust to both distances.

Neither nearsightedness nor farsightedness is healthy for a local church. There needs to be good general vision. When we were missionaries in Liberia, we were fortunate to be supported by some fine mission-minded churches. It was our observation that they didn't separate the mission of the church—reaching people for Jesus Christ—into reaching them either here or there. They were involved in both ends of the field. The sharper the vision of the need to reach all people everywhere, the more effective the ministry of the local church.

## Mission-Minded Churches

When we speak in churches, we often encourage the people to be mission-minded, not just missionary-minded. There is a difference! A missionary-minded church might stop thinking missions when it stops supporting its missionary. It might be

Figure 6

all wrapped up in the missionary's personality and work. But vision must go farther to see the total picture. Christians should see the missionary, the others who are involved in the work, the national church, and the needs of the whole world. The church needs to understand the mission of the church of Jesus Christ around the world to see where they fit in.

We have observed how very important is the vision of the leadership in the mission-minded church. The pastor has a key position. One of our supporting churches was First Baptist Church of Collinsville, Illinois. On our first furlough we met the young pastor and his wife whom we soon learned to love and respect. That couple was Gordon and Gail MacDonald, now pastoring at Grace Chapel in Lexington, Massachusetts. Collinsville was only their second church, but they already knew so much about the world and about missions. Gordon told us, "When I went to seminary, I majored in missions, not to go to the field myself, but to be better able to communicate the mission of the church." He went on to tell Bob that his emphasis for his church was Men and Missions. As he discipled the men of his church, he knew they would take up their responsibilities locally. As he emphasized missions, he saw his church carry out their responsibility for the world. He continues to be known for his dynamic church leadership and as a motivator for missions.

Each year the Collinsville church sent Pastor MacDonald to visit some of their missionaries. Gordon and Gail came to see us in Liberia; and not only did they get a feel of the field to carry back to their church, but they were able to minister to us and to others. The timing was especially good for us because we were going through a time of discouragement. As a husband and wife team, they gave us down-to-earth encouragement. We could laugh with them—and cry with them! Not all churches are able to send their pastors to the mission field. But if they can, it is certainly a benefit for the churches and for the missionaries.

As important as the pastor's leadership is, he is not able to do the job of missions alone. A core of dedicated people can help. Some churches call this a Mission Committee, others a Mission Board. Larger churches can employ a Missions Coordinator or Pastor of Missions. Of encouragement to those carrying out such responsibilities is the growing Association of Church Missions Committees (ACMC), Wheaton, Illinois. Members receive all kinds of helps; resources are pooled, and suggestions are shared.

The formation of a mission policy for the church is a must. This gives direction for decisions to be made. Policies can be set for such matters as the ratio of missionary support for a church member as compared to a nonmember. Criteria can be set for selection of the different types of ministries and agencies to support. Decisions should not depend entirely on the influence of relatives of the candidates, on the charisma of a missionary, or the emotional tug of a service.

The mission committee should oversee the mission education of the church. Mission education is for all ages, with specific goals for the different groups. The biblical basis of missions must be taught. Missionary stories captivate children. Other information comes through films, library books, magazines, and letters from missionaries. World maps show the church's involvement. A mission information center in the foyer is good to keep the church abreast of world mission news. Discussion groups tackle world problems. Weekend seminars can zero in on special ministries or areas of the world. The church can become acquainted with Christian nationals who are visiting or studying here. Maybe a relationship can be built between the church here and a national church. There is excitement in exploring the creative possibilities for mission education!

Then there are special thrusts—mission conferences or festivals which are an educational tool, not an emotional trip. Mission agencies can suggest good ideas for these.

## Producing Missionaries

Do you know where missionaries are produced? Have we been guilty of leaving this job to Christian colleges or Bible schools or other Christian organizations? They help, but it should begin in the local church. It begins with the model that people see for ministry right in the church. What kind of model of church growth, what kind of evangelism model, what ministries of concern do youth see in your local church?

Let's look at the matter of recruitment and selection. Young people today are bombarded with career choices. Vocational counseling in the public schools does not present the opportunities of the mission field. So the church must be all the more certain that this option is placed before young people.

The local church is best suited to see the gifts that people manifest, and to prayerfully approach those who display gifts suitable for missions. This is one area where we feel that the church is often hesitant—to actually be in on the selection process, to call out the "cream of the crop," to personally suggest to someone that he pray about going to a specific place.

This also means that the church has to be aware of the job openings, the opportunities around the world. The mission committee can delegate research to certain members, to evaluate the mission agencies, and thus take active participation in filling vacancies around the world. The church can send youth to missionary conferences such as Inter-Varsity's Urbana, or to summer missions for experience.

For those in the church who are seriously considering going, counseling and encouragement are so important. Some churches have even given financial help for schooling in preparation for going. Young people can be put in a discipleship relationship with older Christians. They can be given practical experience in the church ministries. Some churches have internship programs.

Some missions require that a missionary candidate have cross-cultural experiences in ministry. Churches may not have to look far to provide these experiences. Inner-city ministries or international student ministries offer good opportunities.

Recently when we were in Boston for a Christian Medical Society meeting, Marian took time to go to historic Park Street Church to interview their mission coordinator, Betty Vetterlein, about their missions program. We had been on the receiving end of their vision when we were in Liberia, and missionaries from Park Street have been on the ELWA staff.

As Marian entered the foyer of the church, she saw tables and chairs set up to accommodate the conversational English classes for a group of Asian refugees. Park Street Church doesn't have to look far for cross-cultural ministries. They also have a tremendous ministry to international students—there are some 10,000 in Boston schools. Joe Sabounji, pastor to international students and an international himself, is the coordinator for FOCUS, which stands for Friendship for Overseas College and University Students. It is affiliated with the International Students, Inc. Christian organization.

As the students settle in during September, a big All-American picnic or a banquet welcomes them. Weekly programs continue every Friday evening through the school year, with conversational English classes and special interest groups. Some evenings are for games. Sometimes students are taken to homes. Discussion groups look at current issues, or world cultures, or religions. They might look at what the Bible says about a certain subject. During the year, the foreign students feel a sense of belonging and acceptance in the caring atmosphere at Park Street Church. Some of them come to know Jesus Christ through this friendship program. What an opportunity for this church to do foreign mission work right in Boston!

Working with Joe Sabounji is a team, most of them seminary or college students themselves. This affords an excellent opportunity for cross-cultural ministry for any who are planning to go with missions.

What about the relationship of the church to the mission agency that sends the missionary? It is important that the church trust the mission. The church needs to ask good questions even before the missionary is accepted:

- What is the mission's statement of faith?
- Can the local church agree with it?
- What about the mission leadership?
- What about the financial statement?
- Is their work respected?

Trust is important because the church will have to rely on the mission to evaluate the missionary's day-to-day work on the field. The mission must communicate information they feel would be helpful to the church, and they need to communicate their appreciation of the local church. There needs to be a mutual sense of trust. Good communication is the key.

## The Team Approach
Before we go further, we want to tell you about another way a few churches are getting involved. This is through the team approach. This is a unique cooperative effort, a church-mission partnership. The Elmbrook Church of Waukesha, Wisconsin is a member of such a team.

We had heard something about the vision of this church, but when Bob interviewed Associate Pastor Val Hayworth, coordinator for missions, he found out more. They already are supporting 145 units (each couple or single worker is a unit) as missionaries. Forty of these units are members of Elmbrook Church.

"What is the key to Elmbrook's interest in missions?" Bob asked Pastor Hayworth.

"Our pastor, Stuart Briscoe, has a world vision; that is the key. He passes on to us the world perspective."

But it was the dream of Malcolm Hunter of SIM, who was their missionary-in-residence one year, that Elmbrook might be the instrument to take the Gospel to one unreached people group. Malcolm thought, "Why couldn't this church, in cooperation with a mission agency already working overseas, get involved by supplying the personnel, the finances, and the prayer support to work with one particular group of the unreached?"

That is just what Elmbrook Church is doing. In cooperation with SIM International, they are going to be working with a nomadic group in Kenya, the desert Gabra people of the Borana language. An estimated 150,000 make up this tribal group.

The church is committed to a 20-year project. SIM has researched the people and will give guidelines for beginning the work. Malcolm Hunter, career missionary with SIM and a member of Elmbrook, will continue to work with the project. The goal is to plant among the Gabra people a church which will become part of the national church in Kenya, and in time become a sending church itself.

Of utmost importance has been the selection of personnel from the church membership. The church has been able to assess individual gifts and suitability to the task. The church has a Christian Study Center, a school of missions and theology with subjects at graduate level. This has helped train the team as they are given church responsibilities. The team members are also accepted by SIM as regular missionaries and attend their candidate classes.

"Who are some of the team members?" Bob asked.

"First to go," Pastor Hayworth said, "will be a couple chosen because of their gifts of organization. John was the general manager of a business corporation and in his early 40s. He and his wife, Diane, had lived a social-club, prosperous lifestyle until about eight years ago, when they came to know Christ. Since then their lifestyle has changed considerably, and they have become involved in the church ministries. They will go on ahead and set up the base at Marsabit in Kenya. With John's management skill, business acumen, and maintenance know-how, and with Diane's gift of hospitality, they seemed to be the couple for the base operations and guest house."

Another couple has been chosen for their gifts and training which fit into church planting. A nurse who has taken graduate work at Moody Bible Institute has been selected to head up the community health project. Further down the road, Elmbrook will send out veterinarians, water engineers, agriculturalists, and teachers.

Elmbrook realizes this takes a strong commitment on their part to be a partner in a team relationship. But they are serious about following through on their undertaking, trusting that God will use them in taking the Gospel to the Gabra people so that they might be taken off the "unreached peoples" list.

## The Church's Supportive Role
As church people go to the field, they really can be considered as an extension of the home staff. The local church is the home base for continued encouragement and help. The missionary is accountable to the local church to keep them informed throughout the term. And now on the front line, there's the need for prayer support all the more. Missionaries from Grace Church of Edina in Minneapolis know people are praying, as members of the church make Commitments to Pray for specific workers. The missionaries are mailed a copy of the pledge forms so they know the names of the people on their prayer team.

Coming home on furlough, the missionary may need help in finding housing or in getting a car. We were never fortunate enough to live near our churches that had missionary houses, but we know how much others have appreciated them. Some women have taken missionaries shopping to help them keep up on current fashions. These things help to make the reentry into the American culture easier.

On furlough, missionaries may feel pressured to give a good report and find it hard to share their disappointments, their failures, or really tell their needs. Here's where the mission committee can make it easier by asking insightful questions about the people the missionary is reaching and about the missionary's goals in his work. They can ask about his accomplishments and disappointments. They can ask about his children's needs. They can ask about his plans for the future. Some churches plan to have a Missionary in Residence who can use his or her gifts while on furlough. The missionary may need to stay home for more education, for health needs, or for family needs. The church can give counsel and be supportive in these decisions.

Furlough is a time for relaxation, for reporting, and for busy deputation; but Bob feels that there is another important part. He believes that a missionary should do something—take a course, learn a skill, further his education—that will help him to better himself as a person. The sending church can encourage the missionary to do this.

The mission-minded church sends not only its people but its finances. The mission-minded church finds it impossible to ignore the needs of others around the world, and gets involved with its finances too. There's a sense of responsibility to share what they have.

We know of churches that set as their goal to spend at least as much for missionary outreach as for local ministries. This would seem to be easier for a larger church to do. But recently we also learned of a small church of 100 members that in 1981 gave $27,000 for operational and local ministries and $71,700 for missions!

Some churches give through unified budgets with a certain amount going to missions. Some have separate budgets for general fund and for missions. Others use the Faith Promise

Plan. Through this plan, families or individuals challenged by the needs pray for God's direction in the amount to which they will commit themselves for the coming year for missions. This is in excess of what they will give for the regular support of the church. The promise is an agreement by faith between them and the Lord, and no one contacts them to remind them of this pledge. There are exciting stories of faith at work through the Faith Promise Plan.

Sending churches have so much to share, even from the extras of an abundant lifestyle. During our first year in Liberia, our cement-block house had to be built with gifts that were designated just for that. The shell was up, but it looked like construction was coming to a standstill because the money was running out. One of our churches, Calvary Undenominational Church in Grand Rapids, heard about this and decided to take what they called a "trash offering" to help us finish the house.

For two or three weeks they encouraged their people to go without some of the extras they really didn't need, and instead put the money in some trash barrels at church designated for the offering! They sent over $3,000 for building our house, just enough for us to complete it! This was just from "extras" they could do without! In our happy home in Liberia we were reminded over and over again of their generosity!

We've often thought of that and have wondered just what would happen if all of the churches in America would go without some of the extras and instead give loving offerings for the evangelization of the world! As mission-minded churches become seriously involved in God's mission to the world, as they practice Christian stewardship, finances for missions increase.

# 13

# Where in the World Do You Fit In?

The world is in shaky condition. Political upheaval is the norm. Economic problems cloud the future. World population figures soar. World hunger is a threat. Disasters strike. Nuclear war is possible. The gap continues to widen between the haves and the have-nots. Today the poor know how the rich live and they are restless. Marxism is a threat. Islam is advancing.

But look a little further . . . there is another gap between the haves and the have-nots. Some three billion need yet to hear the Good News of Jesus Christ. There is spiritual unrest in that part of the world.

Jesus said, "Open your eyes and look at the fields! They are ripe for harvest" (John 4:35). Look again at the fields. There are workers out there who are putting in long hours, and new enforcements coming in; but we still see large whitened areas where no one is at work. We must pray that the workers will be sent out to gather the sheaves. Time is running out.

## World Christians

If you are a Christian, then are you a World Christian? We were confronted with this title in David Bryant's book, *In the Gap* (InterVarsity Press). He says there are three steps to becoming a World Christian: you must *catch* a world vision; you must *keep* a world vision, and finally, you must *obey* a world vision.

We put it this way: A World Christian is an *informed* Christian, a *concerned* Christian, and a *responsible* Christian.

• Are you an informed Christian? There really is no excuse not to be informed about the world today. We need to keep up with the news and to be informed about God's work and God's people around the world. We need to be an informed people of God.

• Are you a concerned Christian? Only a cold heart can keep us from being concerned as we look at the world. Compared to others, we are "Gospel affluent" in America. But are we bored by the statistics that tell us of the need of the rest of the world? We must be concerned Christians.

• But a World Christian is not only informed and concerned. He goes the next step and does something about it. He is a responsible Christian.

Sometimes we avoid even thinking that we can have a share in the responsibility of God's mission to the world. It's more comfortable not to think. We may be so caught up with the hectic pace of just living, spinning our wheels, that we can't hear any directions given. It's a noisy culture, and we might not even get quiet enough to listen to God's voice. Do you have a sense of direction in your life, or are you headed the wrong way?

Dr. David Gottas, pastor of the Winnetka Bible Church in Illinois, came to ELWA some years ago on a trip through Africa. Bob really enjoyed visiting with him and offered to drive him to the airport to get his plane to Accra, Ghana. They continued their interesting conversation at the airport. Bob noticed that Dr. Gottas checked through all his luggage, not even a carryon was left.

They sat down in the midst of the confusion of the international airport in Liberia and continued visiting. Then the call came over the loudspeaker announcing a flight on Ghana Airways. They shook hands, said good-bye, and Pastor Gottas was off on the flight.

A couple of days later when Bob was in his busy office at the hospital, a couple of Sierra Leone missionaries stopped by and with a twinkle in their eyes said, "We bring you greetings from Dave Gottas!"

Bob said, "What do you mean? Dave Gottas went to Accra, Ghana!"

Then the missionaries told Bob the story. Dr. Gottas had gotten on the plane, but as it took off and ascended, he noticed that the ocean was on the left side of the plane rather than the right side where it should have been! He was headed west! He was on the wrong plane! He was on the plane to Senegal rather than Accra, Ghana! Two planes were waiting in Liberia, one headed west and the other east. The call came on the loud-speaker for the boarding of the Ghanian Airways plane to Dakar. With all the noise in the airport and his conversation with Bob, Dr. Gottas thought they said to Accra.

He had to wait about four days in Sierra Leone, the country just north of Liberia, until his next flight to Ghana—and without baggage at that! All because he was distracted from listening to the directions!

We wonder how many potential workers aren't out on the field today because they are distracted and aren't listening for any instructions. We wonder how many are seriously considering the options as to where they fit into God's plan.

### Going

Are you one that has looked at the widening gap and seriously considered the option of going? Great! What are the next steps then? First, *get going* in your daily walk, continuing to walk according to Proverbs 3:5-6: "Trust in the Lord with all thine heart: and lean not unto thine own understanding. In all thy ways acknowledge Him, and He shall direct thy paths" (KJV). Move toward a consistent walk with God that says you are willing to do His will. Continue the devotional habit of daily prayer and Bible study.

Next, *stay in contact* with God's people in a good church fellowship. Witness for Jesus Christ right here. Get involved in the church ministries. Look for opportunities to do cross-cultural work and for short-term mission projects.

Next, *keep on going.* Keep on building a world vision. Read books and mission magazines that give exposure to the world's needs and the different ways to go. Contact mission boards and compare their statements of faith, their policies, and their opportunities. Seek counsel from your pastor, missionaries, Christian loved ones, and friends.

If you are a young person still pursuing your education, *prepare* with dedication. Be your best; be ready to go well-prepared. Or maybe it's later in life for you, and you're just going to try a short stint for now. Whatever your age, it will be great to see God direct.

Then, as you move on to the next step, there comes the time to actually *apply* to the mission board. But even after acceptance by the mission, it's the step-by-step walking in His will that finally means going.

Going is an option for the responsible World Christian to consider. Then he listens for God's directions.

## Sending

There's also the option of staying here and sending. It takes a sense of God's direction to stay at home and become a sender. Is that where you fit in God's mission plan?

Dr. Charles Smith, a radiologist from Indiana, his wife, Lee, and their son, Brad, visited us in Liberia. When Dr. Smith was in medical training, he and his wife thought that God was leading them to overseas work. They pursued that course. But then God led otherwise.

Having seriously faced the option of going, the Smiths found it helped them set their priorities here. But they still have a global perspective.

During his last year of training, even before going into a practice, they committed themselves to support of a couple going to West Pakistan. They said they wanted to avoid settling down to lives of relative ease, affluence, and ineffectiveness. The first years were not easy, but they still added more missionaries to the list for support. Seven missionary children have lived with them during college years. Many missionaries have passed through their home.

They also have seen the world at their doorstep. They have been involved in their church, and they have witnessed through Dr. Smith's practice and to their neighborhood. They have had countless Bible studies in their home and have entertained literally thousands of college students for Inter-Varsity college nights. Their perspective is the world, here and there.

Dr. Smith says that he was challenged to set these priorities in 1951 at an Urbana Missionary Convention where he heard speaker Dr. W. Robert Smith say, "Obligating yourself to support someone overseas is the best way I know to maintain your vision for missions and to keep from becoming materialistic as you settle into a job in this country" (Charles Smith, *What If I Don't Go Overseas?* InterVarsity, p. 7).

This speaks of a different lifestyle, a planned lifestyle. We would say this is one of the most difficult things to do as a World Christian in America. Out on the mission field, you know what is expected of you, and there are not so many choices. But here, there are so many choices. A World Christian's lifestyle shows that Jesus Christ is in control of his choices.

Materialism can so easily weight us down. To live a lifestyle of concern requires making the right choices. Think of the choices you make when you try to lose weight. Instead of saying, "I like this food," you have to stick with the choice of, "I should eat this." That's the kind of decision that a concerned Christian makes, reducing the extras that clutter up his life with materialism and distract him from the vision of the world. This results in a reduced lifestyle that frees him up to be a part of God's mission to the world, and frees him up for blessings of involvement like Charles and Lee Smith have had!

Those who go and those who stay are in a team effort. Bob practices general surgery in a group of Christian doctors in Michigan. About half of them are missionary doctors on leave or on furlough from different missions. Others are Christian doctors who are interested in missions and who often go for short-term assignments around the world. Missionary doctors come here to practice during their furloughs. It is a wonderful relationship—a team effort with a world perspective.

That's a picture of the team effort in missions around the world. There are those who stay here to be senders. There are those who come and go, and there are those who spend most of their lives out there. They all fit into God's plan to reach the world.

## Praying

There's one more very important aspect in the life of a World Christian, and that is prayer. This really is not an option. This is a task to which we are called. Are we really serious in our prayer concern for the world?

Earlier we told you of the missionary who visited China shortly after the door there was opened. He told of meeting an unusual Christian woman there. Arrangements were made by others for him to meet her at ten o'clock one evening because her job kept her busy all day. She was 64 years old and for 30 years she had the job of cleaning sewers in China because she was a Christian. All she would have had to say was, "I do not believe in Christ," and she would not have had to clean sewers anymore.

He went that night to meet her, up some backstairs, across a creaking veranda, into a little dark room because all the electricity had gone out. He said, "We sat there. I was expecting this poor little woman to come in and say, 'Oh, it's been awful . . . Ohhh . . . but God has been with me . . . Ohhh . . .'

"But," he said, "pretty soon we heard this *patter, patter, patter* up the stairs . . . *clink, clink, clink* along the veranda. The door burst open, and she came in and asked, 'Who's the missionary?' "

He said, "I am."

She said, "Let me hear you pray!"

He prayed, and she said, "You *are* a missionary!"

Then he said, "Let me hear *you* pray!"

She prayed, and the missionary said, "When she prayed, she brought heaven into that room. She didn't say, 'O Lord, it's been awful . . . where have You been . . . have You been back in the boat sleeping with all these waves around us?' " The missionary continued, "No, she said, 'I thank You for bringing these missionaries,' and she got hold of our hands and prayed her heart out."

The missionary said, "I have never been so humbled in all my life." He asked her, "Can we give you anything?"

And she said, "I only want one thing, a Bible!"

He went back to the hotel, and there was a pastor he knew who was registering. He walked up and said, "Hi!"

The pastor said, "Don't talk to me. I don't want them to know you know me!"

The missionary asked him, "Do you have any Bibles?"

"Yes, I have six."

"Give them to me."

The pastor said, "I can't because when I came across the border they wrote them all down on my passport."

But the missionary said, "Give them to me anyway!" They took all six Bibles, and they cut Matthew, Mark, and Luke out of one, and then they went through all six and made one full Bible. They sewed it together and had a Bible!

The next morning they took it to the Chinese Christian woman, and the pastor still had six Bibles to take back across the border! She said, "This is the greatest thing anyone has ever given to me in my life. How can I thank you enough?" And she started to cry.

The missionary told us, "That woman had learned what we need to learn. She followed Jesus—she counted the cost; she was willing to do anything just so she could follow Jesus."

But her request to the missionary to test his sincerity still rings over and over in our ears—*"Let me hear you pray!"*

What would she say if she could hear our prayers? Out across the world today are others without any Bibles, others without even the message of hope that we have, the nearly three billion who do not have a witness. If they could hear us pray, what would they say?

We do not begin to realize what could be accomplished through prayer. Jesus told us to pray. Are we sincerely praying for His mission to be carried out to the ends of the earth? That humble Chinese woman's words remind us that our Lord Jesus Christ is also saying, "Let Me hear you pray."

Today millions are being mobilized to pray daily for the hidden people—the unreached people—around the world. We sense that World Christians are getting serious about their commitment to pray.

Today there is the anticipation of a great thrust of workers into the fields ready for harvest. More manpower is available than ever before, with more job opportunities opening. There are more methods to use. We have modern means—the latest in technology—at our disposal. As we come to the countdown of the twentieth century, we know that the great day is drawing closer when the redeemed of the Lord will stand before His throne, "a great multitude that no one could count, from every nation, tribe, people, and language" (Rev. 7:9). What a day that will be!

The evangelization of the world: An impossible task? With God it is possible, as World Christians fit into His plan and carry out His strategy to reach the yet unreached for Jesus Christ. Where do you fit in?

# Bibliography

Adeney, David H. *Christian Students Face the Revolution.* Downers Grove, Ill.: InterVarsity Press, 1973.

Bailey, Faith Coxe. *Adoniram Judson.* Chicago: Moody Press, 1955.

Broomhall, Marshall. *Hudson Taylor, The Man Who Believed God.* London: China Inland Mission, 1929.

Bryant, David. *In the Gap: What It Means to Be a World Christian.* Downers Grove, Ill.: InterVarsity Press, 1981.

Coggins, Wade T. *So That's What Missions Is All About.* Chicago: Moody Press, 1975.

Cowart, John W. "The Story of Saint Patrick," *HIS.* Downers Grove, Ill.: InterVarsity Press: March 1980.

Dayton, Edward R. *That Everyone May Hear.* Monrovia, Calif.: MARC, 1980.

Deyneka, Anita & Peter. "A Salvation of Suffering," *Christianity Today.* Carol Stream, Ill.: vol. 26, no. 12, 1982.

_____. *Song in Siberia.* Elgin, Ill.: David C. Cook, 1977.

Drewery, Mary. *William Carey.* Grand Rapids: Zondervan, 1979.

Elder, John. *The Biblical Approach to the Muslim.* Fort Washington, Penn.: World Evangelization Crusade, 1978.

Engstrom, Ted W. *What in the World Is God Doing? The New Face of Missions.* Waco, Texas: Word Books, 1978.

Everswick, Dale. "We Can't Take Tomorrow for Granted," *TEAM Horizons.* Wheaton, Ill.: vol. 58, no. 4, 1982.

Frizen, Edwin L, Jr., & Coggins, Wade T., eds. *Christ and Caesar in Christian Missions.* Pasadena, Calif.: William Carey Library, 1979.

Fry, C. George, and King, James R. *Islam—A Survey of the Muslim Faith.* Grand Rapids: Baker, 1980.

Fuller, W. Harold. *Mission-Church Dynamics.* Pasadena, Calif.: William Carey Library, 1980.

Griffiths, Michael. *The Church & World Mission.* Grand Rapids: Zondervan, 1982.

Hall, Clarence W. *Miracle on the Sepik.* Costa Mesa, Calif.: Gift Publications, 1980.

Hay, Ian M. *Now Why Did I Do That? The Biblical Basis of Motivation.* Scarborough, Ont.: SIM, 1977.

Hillis, Don. "Honey, Locusts, and Hairy Garments," *WHEREV-ER.* Wheaton, Ill.: TEAM, Fall 1981.

Howard, David M., ed. *Declare His Glory Among the Nations.* Downers Grove, Ill.: InterVarsity Press, 1977.

_____. *Student Power in World Evangelism.* Downers Grove, Ill.: InterVarsity Press, 1970.

Hulbert, Terry C. *World Missions Today.* Wheaton, Ill.: Evangelical Teacher Training Association, 1981.

*In Other Words, Jubilee.* Huntington Beach, Calif.: Wycliffe, vol. 7, no. 6, 1981.

Johnstone, Patrick J. *Operation World.* Waynesboro, Ga.: STL Publications, 1980.

Kane, J. Herbert. *A Global View of Missions.* Grand Rapids: Baker, 1971.

_____. *The Christian World Mission: Today and Tomorrow.* Grand Rapids: Baker, 1981.

_____. *The Making of a Missionary.* Grand Rapids: Baker, 1975.

_____. *Understanding Christian Missions.* Grand Rapids: Baker, 1974.

_____. *Winds of Change in the Christian Mission.* Grand Rapids: Baker, 1973.

Kauffman, Paul E. *CHINA, The Emerging Challenge: A Christian Perspective.* Grand Rapids: Baker, 1982.

Keyes, Lawrence E. *The Last Age of Missions.* Pasadena, Calif.: William Carey Library, 1983.

Lageer, Eileen. *New Life for All.* Chicago: Moody Press, 1970.

Lausanne Occasional Papers. *Thailand Report—Christian Witness to Refugees—Christian Witness to the Chinese People—Christian Witness to Large Cities.* Wheaton, Ill.: LCWE, 1980.

Lenning, Larry G. *Blessing in Mosque and Mission.* Pasadena, Calif.: William Carey Library, 1980.

Loss, Myron. *Culture Shock.* Winona Lake, Ind.: Light and Life Press, 1983.

Lovering, Kerry. "Assignment: Gola!" *AFRICA NOW.* Cedar Grove, N.J.: SIM, no. 106, 1979.

———. *Islam: Bid for Renewal.* Scarborough, Ont.: SIM, 1978.

———. *Islam: On the March.* Scarborough, Ont.: SIM, 1979.

McCurry, Don M., ed. *The Gospel and Islam: A 1978 Compendium.* Monrovia, Calif.: MARC, 1979.

McDowell, Josh, and Stewart, Don. *Understanding Non-Christian Religions.* San Bernardino, Calif.: Here's Life Publishers, 1982.

Marsh, C. R. *Share Your Faith with a Muslim.* Chicago: Moody Press, 1975.

Miller, Doug. "Taking a Treasure to Tree-Dwellers," *WHEREVER.* Wheaton, Ill.: TEAM, vol. 5, no. 3, 1980.

Miller, William M. *A Christian's Response to Islam.* Wheaton, Ill.: Tyndale House, 1980.

Nelson, Marlin L., ed. *Readings in Third World Missions: A Collection of Essential Documents.* South Pasadena, Calif.: William Carey Library, 1976.

Parshall, Phil. *New Paths in Muslim Evangelism.* Grand Rapids: Baker, 1980.

Peters, George W. *A Biblical Theology of Missions.* Chicago: Moody Press, 1972.

*Reaching Muslims Today.* Upper Darby, Penn.: North Africa Mission, 1976.

Roddy, Lee. *On Wings of Love.* Nashville: Thomas Nelson Publishers, 1981.

Smith, Charles. *What If I Don't Go Overseas?* Downers Grove, Ill.: InterVarsity Press, 1981.

Steering Committee. *New Directions and Opportunities for Chris-*

*tian Health Care Ministries.* Wheaton, Ill.: MAP, Int., 1982.

Taylor, Dr. and Mrs. Howard. *J. Hudson Taylor, God's Man in China.* Chicago: Moody Press, 1982.

Traub, Margaret. "Relief for the Oppressed in the Village Called Africa," *Christianity Today.* Carol Stream, Ill.: vol. 23, no. 19, 1979.

Troutman, Charles. *Everything You Want to Know about the Mission Field, but Are Afraid You Won't Learn Until You Get There.* Downers Grove, Ill.: InterVarsity Press, 1976.

————. "Steps to Mature Servanthood Overseas," *Evangelical Missions Quarterly.* Wheaton, Ill.: vol. 19, no. 1, 1983.

Tucker, Ruth A. *From Jerusalem to Irian Jaya.* Grand Rapids: Zondervan, 1983.

Wagner, C. Peter. *Frontiers in Missionary Strategy.* Chicago: Moody Press, 1972.

Wagner, C. Peter, & Dayton, Edward R., eds. *Unreached Peoples '81.* Elgin, Ill.: David C. Cook, 1981.

————. *On the Crest of the Wave.* Ventura, Calif.: Regal, 1983.

————. *Stop the World. I Want to Get On.* Glendale, Calif.: Regal, 1973.

Wakatama, Pius. *Independence for the Third World Church.* Downers Grove, Ill.: InterVarsity Press, 1976.

Williams, Theodore. "Missionaries: What Kind?" *Frontier Fellowship.* Wheaton, Ill.: WEF Edition, November 1982

Wilson, J. Christy. *Today's Tentmakers.* Wheaton, Ill.: Tyndale, 1978.

Wilson, Samuel, ed. *Mission Handbook: North American Protestant Ministries Overseas.* 12th Edition, Monrovia, Calif.: MARC, 1979.

Winter, Ralph D., and Hawthorne, Steven C., eds. *Perspectives on the World Christian Movement.* Pasadena, Calif.: William Carey Library, 1981.

*Your Muslim Guest.* Toronto: Fellowship of Faith for Muslims, 1978.